HOW TO

MAKE MONEY TYPING

VOLUME I

By
Diane E. Robinson

Published By

Clarendon House

Library of Congress Catalog Card Number: 95-909771

ISBN 1-886908-05-2
1st Edition

Printed in the United States of America

Acknowledgments

We would like to take this opportunity to thank the many people involved in the development and publication of *How to Make Money Typing*. The guidance, inspiration and constant encouragement of the following organizations and people made this book possible: the dedicated team of mentors of SCORE (Service Corps of Retired Executives), the SBA (Small Business Administration), the United States Chamber of Commerce, and the University of California Reference Librarians.

A very special thank you to the legion of pioneering entrepreneurs who have created the home-office revolution. It is because of these independent thinkers that working at home has become an accepted way of doing business.

A Note from the Publisher

We have made every effort to ensure the accuracy of the information in this book. However, we cannot be held responsible for any errors that may have inadvertently been made, or for changes in any of the information since we went to print. The book is designed to provide information about starting and operating a home-based typing business, and is sold with the understanding that the author and publisher are not in any way engaged in, or offering accounting, marketing, legal or any other professional services. In all such matters we recommend that you seek the services of a competent professional.

Trademark names appear throughout this book and rather than inserting the registered trademark symbol with every mentioned name, the publisher declares that they are only using those names for editorial and informational purposes, with no intentional infringement upon the trademark. Please always bear in mind that our sole purpose in writing this book is to inform and help you, the reader.

Table of Contents

Foreword

We're delighted that you have chosen to invest in this book! We also think you'll find *How to Make Money Typing* one of the most complete books of its kind available today, a reference resource that you will use many times.

The information contained in this book represents a wealth of opportunity for anyone wanting to join the home-based business revolution. Our researchers have found the latest in equipment, communications and marketing information that will enable you to set up and run a home-based typing business.

Just as any business venture requires dedication and motivation, we believe that consulting this book will help you make the right decisions, based on the information provided. And while this book can make your professional life easier, it is only the beginning of your exciting journey to successful entrepreneurship.

Use this book as your coach, guide, and mentor, and you'll be on your way to creating a home-based typing business that meets *your* needs!

The Publisher

Introduction

Since you have this book in your hands and are obviously interested in starting your own typing/word-processing business, it seems only fair to assume this is something you would like to do. Well, the good news is ..... *action follows thought!* You've taken action after thinking about what you might like to accomplish, and this book is the next step to putting your thoughts into motion.

Never in human history has there been more opportunity for an individual to create a successful business from the privacy of their own home. According to *Entrepreneur Magazine*, someone starts a home-based business every eleven seconds! With the explosion and affordability of the personal computer, the Fax machine and the information superhighway, it is now possible to conduct the same type of business that once was the highly guarded secret of mega corporations. If you can sit in a high-rise office building and type a sales report, memo, letter, etc., *you can now sit at home, in your home office, and do the very same thing!*

The U.S. Labor Department predicts that by the year 2000, up to one half of all Americans could be working from their home offices. That's tens of millions of people just like you! Many will be home-based employees of major corporations, but millions more will be home-based entrepreneurs running their own businesses. The time to begin laying the foundation for your future success is *NOW!*

Perhaps the best news is that almost anyone can begin a home-based typing business. Of course, it is most helpful if you already know how to type, and even more advantageous if you have computer-based word processing skills, but the truth is ... those skills can be learned. If you've been away from the working world for some time and your skills are rusty, you can always take a refresher course through your local adult education program or community college. Another way to update your skills and knowledge if you feel the need is to sign on with a temporary employment agency.

If, for instance, you accepted a 30-day temporary assignment and all you did was straight typing, I guarantee your typing speed and accuracy would improve by probably 50%! And, you'd be getting paid to acquire or update the skills necessary to start your business.

The real measure of your success will ultimately depend on how much effort and time you choose to put into your business. Are you looking for the freedom to work around family responsibilities? Are you fed up with corporate politics, layoffs, stagnant pay and a lack of upward mobility? I sure was. Have you ever dreamed of being your own boss and being rewarded strictly on the basis of your ability, dedication and work? There's nothing in the world like having roses delivered to your door, thanks from a grateful client with the "rush" job. Or the satisfaction that comes from knowing that you, and only you, are responsible for that job well done.

The primary reason most people start a home-based business is a desire to improve the quality of their home and family life. Don't believe everything you've heard about working at home as a self- employed person. The truth is, almost everyone who has chosen this type of lifestyle loves it! Any chosen career or activity is worthwhile if:

- It brings you a positive response
- What you do helps other people
- You believe that it is worth doing
- You feel good while you're doing the work
- You make a good income doing the work

While there are no guarantees that any type of work will bring you all of these rewards immediately, experience proves that you will most certainly achieve at least two or three, and quite possibly all of the above over time.

If you've begun to resent the hour-long commute, the added expense of working in an office (pantyhose, clothes, lunches), not to mention the auto-related costs of getting there and back, perhaps the time is right for you to become one of America's 39 million home-based workers.

I knew it was time for me to find another way to earn a living when after completing a grueling year-end budget project my boss said to me at three o'clock on Friday afternoon, "Good job. You can take the rest of the day off." I knew that he was going to get a big bonus for finishing on time, and I'd also heard that his boss was sending him and his wife to Hawaii ... *all expenses paid!* I fumed all weekend. It just wasn't fair. Finally my husband said "Quit complaining and do something about it!" Well I did, and as you're about to find out, becoming a home-based business owner was the smartest thing I've ever done. If it worked for me, it can work for you!

Let's take a moment to evaluate your professional experience and skills. Using the chart on the next page, circle your skill level for each task from 1 to 5: 1 meaning little or no experience, 5 being very skilled in that particular task. Use the results to help you evaluate the areas of interest that you want to work in, and also to pinpoint certain skills that you may want to brush up on.

Professional Skill Evaluation Checklist

Typing	1	2	3	4	5
Word Processing	1	2	3	4	5
Filing	1	2	3	4	5
Telephone Skills	1	2	3	4	5
Data Entry	1	2	3	4	5
Shorthand	1	2	3	4	5
Transcription	1	2	3	4	5
Bookkeeping	1	2	3	4	5
Self Motivation	1	2	3	4	5
Marketing	1	2	3	4	5
Working under Pressure	1	2	3	4	5
Other Skills	1	2	3	4	5
_____	1	2	3	4	5
_____	1	2	3	4	5
_____	1	2	3	4	5
_____	1	2	3	4	5
_____	1	2	3	4	5
_____	1	2	3	4	5

Is working as a home-based typist the right choice for you? We'll discuss it in more detail later, but for now ask yourself these questions. They will help you confirm that you're on the right track and help you decide how to get the ball rolling!

Do I need to generate full or part-time income from my typing business? _____

Do I have a small area in my home where I can work productively? _____

Do I have the support of my friends, business associates and family? _____

Do I have the few necessary office supplies and equipment to begin working? _____

Am I able to read, study and develop the necessary discipline required to make my business a success? _____

If you answered yes to all five questions, congratulations! You've been thinking about and preparing for this longer than you imagine. If you were unsure of some of the questions, that's OK too. It simply means you have a little homework to do to get ready to hang out your shingle.

Chapter 1: Overview and Fast Start

This chapter is designed to give you an overview of the contents of this book—and by doing so, to help you get started in your very own typing/word processing business that much sooner!

The good news is, you'll find that starting a typing/word processing business is really not difficult at all. You just need to become familiar with the steps and procedures involved. That's where this book comes in. Use this chapter as a guide to its contents. When you come across a topic that is especially interesting to you, then simply turn to that chapter to learn more.

If you're not sure what a typing business involves, there's no better place to start than **Chapter 2: What Is a Home-Based Typing Business?** This chapter explains the difference between typing and word processing, and why you shouldn't be intimidated if you haven't yet joined the Computer Age. The similarities between being a personal secretary and running an independent typing/word processing business are discussed.

Then Chapter 2 goes on to explore the many types of clients you can expect to find for your new business. Did you know that there are five major categories of clients for home-based typing—business and corporate, medical, legal, academic, and literary—*plus one other little-known category that can be an excellent source of income for you!* You'll also find a chart to fill out that will get you thinking about all the people you know who could be potential clients for your new business venture. This chapter concludes with a list of 50 more businesses that could possibly use your typing services!

Chapter 3, Where to Get Training, will explain exactly how to get started in your new career—even if you don't know how to type! You'll learn about business schools, transcription, spreadsheets, how to build a niche for yourself, and much more. You'll learn that high school typing alone is oftentimes enough training to get started. Plus, you'll find out why you probably don't have to worry about carpal tunnel syndrome!

Chapters 4-7 take you on an in-depth tour of some of the most profitable areas available to you as a home-based typist. Pick the chapters that interest you the most and read on for more exciting information! Choose from **Chapter 4, Resumes; Chapter 5, Medical Typing; Chapter 6, Legal Typing; or Chapter 7, Desktop Publishing.** You'll soon see why the sky's the limit for you and your new business!

Chapter 8, Getting Ready for Success, lists the steps you'll need to follow to get your home-based typing business up and running. For inspiration, you'll find the story of Nancy Browning here, a single mother of two who started her own successful business on a shoestring. If you're wondering exactly how well suited you are to running a business, fill out the questionnaire in this chapter and rate your responses. Chances are you'll find that you're more ready than you thought!

Also in Chapter 8, you'll learn an easy method of creating a business plan that will make you wonder why you didn't do it sooner! Then, you'll find out how to estimate the start-up costs for your business. What if you don't have the cash? Not to worry—there are many options available that will get your doors open for business no matter what! *You'll discover three action plans to start your business now, and a list of other financing options that you may not have thought of yet.* Finally, you'll learn the answers to two very important questions: how much money do I need to make, and how much should I charge?

Now you're ready to make your dream a reality! **Chapter 9, Things To Do,** takes you through the practical steps of getting your business off on the right foot. First and among the most fun of these steps is to name your business! You'll learn what a Fictitious Business Name statement is, and weigh the pros and cons of using your own name for your business versus a made-up name. You'll also learn how SCORE (Service Corps of Retired Executives) and the SBA (Small Business Administration) can help you get your business started.

Ever wonder if you need to get a business license—and how to do it? You'll find out how in Chapter 9. And don't forget the other nuts and bolts, like opening a business checking account (and why you need to separate your personal and business checking), what to do when a customer's check bounces, business taxes, business cards and stationery—*it's all here, plus why it's a good idea to let everyone you do business with know that you're a new business owner.*

Chapter 10, Your Working Environment, delves into the subject of setting up your home office. When you work at home, you automatically get benefits such as lower daily expenses and tax write-offs for your home office. These perks are great, but you also need to develop some new coping skills for working at home. This chapter talks about how to develop self-discipline, and especially the importance of training your family to respect your need for privacy. *Then, by answering four simple questions, you'll be able to make some important decisions about your work schedule and productivity.* You'll even find ten time-tested ideas for keeping your working hours productive and profitable!

Then Chapter 10 goes on to talk about creating your work space—*and why the most important feature of your new home office is the door!* You'll learn why it's so important to find a space that's totally separate from the rest of your house and your daily life. But at the same time, adding personal touches that enable you to relax in your work space is a great idea. Your home office can, and should, be a reflection of who you are as a person—and a place where you and your clients feel totally comfortable and at home. You'll find many helpful suggestions here to make your work space the best it can be!

By now you might be wondering exactly what equipment you need for your new business! **Chapter 11, Choosing Your Equipment,** covers this topic in detail. First on the list is the right telephone service and an answering machine—a device that can really save you time and money! Next, you might want to consider a Fax machine. With prices going down on Fax machines all the time, this is truly a great investment for your business—but there are many local businesses that offer Fax services to individuals just like you. This chapter has all the details.

What about a copy machine? The pros and cons of making this substantial investment are also covered in Chapter 11. Last, but not least, there remains the question of what kind of equipment you'll be typing on—an electric typewriter, a dedicated word processor, or a computer? The remain-

der of this chapter weighs the advantages and disadvantages of each. *You won't want to invest in any one of these three options until you read this important information!*

Now you're ready to let people know about your new business! **Chapter 12, Advertising, Marketing, and Public Relations,** offers you the keys to success in each of these three important areas. Each one is defined and discussed in detail. You'll learn what kinds of advertising work best for typing/word processing businesses, which newspapers to advertise in, and other publications that might work well for you. Whether or not to advertise in the Yellow Pages of your local phone book is covered here, plus other advertising options you can create yourself like flyers, newsletters, and brochures.

Can you imagine advertising your typing/word processing service on radio and cable TV? You can find great deals at local radio and TV stations, so don't rule out this little-used way to let an incredible number of people know about your business! The how-tos are covered in Chapter 12. You'll also learn about the importance of networking and cold calling when it comes to discovering potential new clients—and how easy both are to do! This chapter concludes with a look at the wonderful opportunities you can generate for free advertising via an effective public relations campaign. Using the sample press release provided, you're all set to make your business known to the local media!

Once your business is under way, how do you keep customers coming back for more? **Chapter 13, Customer Service,** explores the secrets of making customers happy—and keeping them that way. You'll learn why it's important to adopt a can-do attitude, as well as being flexible and expanding the services you offer. You'll discover the importance of greeting your customers with enthusiasm and making them feel welcome at all times. *It's not all smoke and mirrors, but a special trick that involves using a mirror when you answer the phone can really help you improve your phone manner!*

Chapter 13 also covers what to do when customers make you miserable, the importance of remaining calm at all times, and the warning signs of a customer you can never satisfy. *Then you'll discover the secret of how to get rid of a problem client with ease!* When ethical questions pop up, this chapter will help guide you to the right decision. You'll learn the importance of honesty, integrity, and being able to say "I'm sorry." Then you'll find tips on how to handle deadlines and build a portfolio that you can use to go out and solicit more business. Finally, if you've ever wondered how you might handle the rejection and isolation that can be a part of working at home, this chapter will give you coping strategies that really work!

As your business grows and develops over time, you'll experience a turnover in clients for a variety of reasons. *How do you maintain an adequate customer base?* The answer to this important question is found in **Chapter 14, Finding and Keeping Customers.** You'll discover the magic that can happen when a client asks you to do something that you've never done before and say yes—and then you actually make it happen! This kind of professional growth is one of the keys to finding and keeping customers.

Another important factor in finding new customers is networking. In its broadest sense, this word refers to the entire network of relationships in your life—in fact, you can find practically unlimited opportunities to expand your business all around you, every day! Chapter 14 will show you how. You'll learn the importance of keeping in touch with your best customers, too. It's all part of making yourself, and your services, indispensable!

And what about the rewards you get for your hard work and dedication to customer service? Turn to **Chapter 15, Making Money and Getting Paid,** for insights into this all-important topic! Remember, you didn't go into business to go broke. This chapter tells you how to price your services, how to evaluate what your business is costing you, when to raise your prices, *and why the Ten Percent Rule is the key to your financial security!*

You'll also be reminded about the importance of setting clear policies and terms by which to run your business—how to handle phone inquiries and price quotes, how to request deposit agreements, and whether to accept cash, checks, or credit. Finally, Chapter 15 gives you a proven method of finding out what your customers really think about you and your business!

What do you do when your business starts to take over your life? That's when it's time to consult **Chapter 16, Keeping It All Together.** The art of keeping your work life and home life in balance is covered in this very important chapter. When you're working for yourself, all of a sudden it can seem like you're working all the time! This chapter has creative ideas and suggestions to help keep your life in perspective and your business on track.

Don't forget that all great ideas need time to be nurtured—and your typing/word processing business is no exception! The **Conclusion** of this book reminds you to take your time assimilating all of this important information. As the economy continues to change and more people start working from their homes, you'll find yourself in good company when you decide the time is right to start earning your living by home-based typing! *One thing's for sure—it's an adventure and challenge that you won't want to miss!*

At the end of this book, you'll find a helpful list of **Resources** to guide you on your way. These include associations that exist especially to help new business people such as yourself, as well as magazines and other publications that you can either consult at your local library or subscribe to yourself. This book concludes with a **Glossary** so you can identify any unfamiliar phrases you might come across in this book or other reading material.

With so many resources out there to learn more about starting your own business, you can always rest assured that you'll find the answers to your questions quickly and easily. In short, there's a world of opportunity awaiting you and your new typing/word processing business. You'll never know how great it feels to be your own boss until you try it! So use this book as your guide, and remember that *you too* can make it happen. Good luck!

Chapter 2:
What Is a Home-Based Typing Business?

The United States Chamber of Commerce recently reported that of the fifteen million businesses that filed IRS Schedule C (Sole Proprietor), ten million listed their home address as their place of business. As the need for information processing grows, the opportunities for you to develop long-term client relationships also grows.

Right now, many major companies are arranging for their employees or independent contractors (that means you!) to take up the increasing work load. Skilled typists who can produce letter-perfect documents on time, and at a reasonable rate are in constant demand. But it's not only large companies who need your services—think of your doctor or medical group, as well as attorneys, professors, writers, and students with term papers due. *Everyone has something that needs to be typed.*

In other words, a typing service takes raw, written material and turns it into a perfectly formatted, correctly spelled document.

A Word About Word Processing

What's the difference between straight typing and word processing? It's simple, really. The basic keyboard entry of words, paragraphs and sentences is the same. But when a typed document needs to be corrected because of spelling or content changes, word processing allows you to recall the information from a storage system that's incorporated into your equipment. The material you've already typed is displayed on the video screen of your computer or word processor, and you can then make changes easily and print out the new version. The term word processor refers to a personal computer that is "dedicated" to the task of word processing and can perform no other function. Computer-based desktop publishing programs also contain word processing features.

There are many memory equipped electronic typewriters and dedicated word processors on the market today (we will discuss the different types of systems and equipment in Chapter 11, Choosing Your Equipment), and there is absolutely no reason why you cannot start your typing service with such equipment, but it is not recommended that you begin such an undertaking with the old-fashion standard manual typewriter. It would be like trying to climb an icy mountain barefoot in your shorts!

Don't worry if you haven't quite made it all the way into the computer age, or traveled down the information superhighway. I was terrified of the whole idea of having to become "computer literate," but I learned that if you just take it step by step, and try not to look too far into the future, you'll be just fine. Even if you decide to jump into the computer maze at a later date, every skill you develop now will help you even more in your work. Take your time and try not to be overwhelmed by thinking about the "what ifs."

To put it quite simply, a typing/word processing service does whatever a personal secretary would do ..... only you do it for many businesses and individuals at one time. From consultants to market research firms to law offices, the independent typist/word processor functions as an office away from home. In addition to routine reports and letters, your service may also offer resume and job search cover letters, newsletters, direct mail sales materials, book manuscripts—the list goes on and on. The kinds of documents that need to be typed are endless! There are:

Five Major Categories for Home-Based Typing

1. Business and Corporate

This will probably be your greatest source of business and income, as companies of every description need to hire extra typing/word processing services at one time or another. Even if you are an experienced secretary, make sure your skills and corporate etiquette are up to date. If you're just getting started in the business world it would be a good idea to invest in a secretarial manual that when kept right at your fingertips will answer all of your questions about how to format business letters, reports, etc.

Because there are so many different types of businesses, there are just as many types of jobs that could come your way. Susie Preston left the high pressure and daily deadlines of the newspaper world when her first son was born. As an input typist for the advertising department, it was her job to set the type for the hundreds of ads that were placed in the newspaper every day. She had been in her position for over four years, and the low salary combined with high daycare costs started her thinking that she could easily do this from home while taking care of her son.

Because she had gotten to know almost all of the advertisers, she had a great client base ready to send her typing as soon as she got her home office set up. That was almost ten years ago! Susie now has four sons, and says she would never go back to working away from home.

2. Medical

This area can include transcription as well as typing. If you are a qualified, experienced transcriptionist you will certainly want to include that service as it is in great demand on an independent basis.

Areas almost always open to home-based typists include typing consulting reports and case studies, transcribing and typing pathology findings, filling out insurance claim forms, typing trade journal articles and speeches. In this field as well as the legal field, confidentiality is of the utmost importance as the medical profession is greatly concerned with malpractice issues and violation of the doctor/patient relationship.

3. Legal

Although one of the most lucrative and greatest sources of potential business for your typing service, research indicates that some experience in the field working as a legal secretary is necessary. You could probably pick up some routine correspondence typing from independent attorneys, but this could be a difficult area to break into if you don't know the lingo!

If you do have prior experience, you may even want to consider specializing your typing service to only include law. Transcribing notes for deposition services and court reporters offers another potential source of income while working in the same field and learning the ropes. Many of today's court reporters are now computer equipped so it could be that sporadic overload or rush jobs would be offered to you as an independent typist.

4. Academic

Teachers today are overburdened and have little time to type! In addition, because of budget cuts the clerical staffing at most institutions is nowhere near what it used to be. Schools, universities, students, and administrators will all be a potential source of business for you.

Think about the old adage in academia, "Publish or Perish"! Then think about how a professor's manuscript must be typed and be letter-perfect before he can submit it to a publisher. But that's only the beginning. Think of all the people going back to school to further their education who must write term papers, reports, outlines, essays, theses, etc.

Every one of these items must be typed before it can be turned in. Another source of business for you will be private institutions, pre-schools, religious and military academies. All privately funded institutions must communicate with donors and parents through fund raising solicitation letters, newsletters and scholarship information.

Perhaps it's time to sit down with pen and notebook and make a list of every potential business or organization you have contact with. Your church, bank, PTA, pre-school, health club—these and many more are included in the list of 50 potential clients you'll find at the end of this chapter. All of these businesses and organizations need to communicate with their customers by letter, flyer, brochure, etc. Think about the amount of mail you receive regarding sales, fund raisers, club news, loan programs. Each and every organization has to communicate with their customers, and all of that information has to be typed before it can be sent out. You might as well be the one to type it!

5. Literary

Writers are not necessarily good typists! Nor are they especially good at objectively editing their own creative work. Although many writers do work on some sort of word processing or computer equipment, many still want to write in longhand or talk into a recorder and have their material transcribed.

When you consider that most people begin a writing career after they retire, it's easy to understand why they don't want to learn how to type—they want to write! Understanding that most writers don't make much money from their writing, this may not be the biggest money-maker on your client list, but for sheer volume (and perhaps increasing your typing skills and speed) those poor tortured souls churning out plays, novels, T.V. and movie scripts will be a steady source of income. And the work is always interesting to read.

Now I'm going to add one more category of potential clients that most home-based typists tend to overlook because they don't fully understand the nature of:

Non-Profit Organizations

The term non-profit doesn't necessarily mean the organization has no money— it just means they are required to account for every single penny they spend! This growing segment of our society encompasses every social area including providing assistance to children, foreign countries, senior citizens, religious organizations, etc. The list is endless.

These organizations are often understaffed and rely on volunteers to run things on a local, and sometimes national level. Their typing needs may include donor solicitation letters, mailing labels and lists, newsletters, awards, public service announcements, etc. Often times these charitable groups cannot afford to hire on-staff clerical help and this is where your typing service comes in.

Not only are non-profits abundant in number, they often share information with other agencies. So if you are hired to type a donor letter for the Red Cross, it's quite possible that their director will tell the director of Family Services about you and your service. Another bonus comes in getting your name and business affiliated with social and charitable causes. This type of promotion and name recognition is great for your business!

Make Your Own Client List

The six categories of clients described above are only the beginning. Right now, go get your Yellow Pages phone book. Begin looking at the many different types of businesses and organizations. This should jog your thinking process as to the thousands of opportunities right in your own home town that could utilize your service. *Start making a list right now by filling in the names of the people you do business with:*

My Potential Client List

Bank _____

Insurance Co. _____

Schools _____

Doctor _____

Lawyer _____

Dentist _____

Jeweler _____

Auto dealer _____

Newspaper _____

Friends & Relatives in Business _____

_____

_____

As you become more proficient and gather more diverse clients, the opportunities to expand your typing services will continue to grow. For example, just think for one moment of the many things you can do with a home-based typing business:

- Offer Technical And Scientific Word Processing
- Provide Direct Mail Marketing
- Perform Book Indexing
- Write A Classified Ad Newsletter

- Collect Quotes And Jokes For Speechwriters
- Create Form Letters
- Offer Foreign Language Word Processing
- Write Personalized Children's Books
- Generate and Sell Mailing Lists
- Offer Letter Writing Services
- Provide A Resume Service
- Prepare Business Proposals
- Sell Mailing Labels

Literally, the services you can offer through your typing business are unlimited! Find the things that interest you and make them a part of what you do to earn your living every day. This advice is probably among the best I ever received. I suggest you seriously consider it.

50 More Potential Clients for Your Home-Based Typing Business

Advertising Agencies

Busy advertising agencies have many typing needs, from press releases to newsletters, brochures, and more! You could be the right-hand typing professional they turn to in a deadline crunch, and once they know and trust you, they'll send many projects your way!

Amusement Parks

If you live near even a small amusement park, this can be a potential gold mine for you! Amusement parks are always passing out flyers and coupons for special offers—and someone needs to type them. It might as well be you, and this can be one of your most entertaining clients!

Answering Service Bureaus

Oftentimes these service bureaus offer a full range of office services to their clients. You could end up being a personal secretary to a wide range of clients who find out about you through the service bureau. Get to know the owners and put networking to work for you!

Antique Dealers

If you have a special interest in antiques, you could drum up business for local dealers by getting to know them at their places of business. They usually have extensive correspondence that must be typed, as well as inventories, sales lists, advertising flyers, and much more!

Apartment Managers

If you live in a large apartment complex, you may find your best client very close to home in the form of your apartment manager! There's an incredible amount of paperwork involved with any kind of management, and you can use this opportunity to make yourself indispensable!

Appraisers

These individuals determine the value of items ranging from real estate and cars to fine jewelry and antiques. Here's an opportunity to cultivate a great business client with needs for correspondence, official documents, and other essential items that need typing by someone like you!

Architects

Even a small architectural firm needs typing help when it's time to get out a proposal on the next big project. If you've always been fascinated by how buildings get built, you'll probably find this work extremely interesting!

Art Galleries

Every time an art gallery has a show, they send out postcards to their entire mailing list—just think of all that typing! If you like art, here's your chance to be around a stimulating environment and make good money typing as well!

Boat Dealers

If you live near the water, check out the opportunities for your typing service among the boat dealers and other businesses that serve the waterfront community. From record-keeping to flyers, you're sure to find plenty of work to keep you busy!

Bookstores

There are many kinds of bookstores besides the big chains in your local mall. Check out the rare and antiquarian bookstores in your community. They all need help with correspondence and record-keeping. Even used bookstores may have the need for occasional typing help.

Business Fairs

Most communities have business fairs several times a year sponsored by local organizations like the Chamber of Commerce. Attend these fairs with your best business attire and a pile of business cards. Meet all the exhibitors and pass out your cards—or even better, be an exhibitor yourself!

Career Counselors

Did you know that some individuals make a business out of career counseling? These are usually highly educated people who use their training to help people find new jobs and plan the rest of their lives. And they need accurate, reliable typing help to make sure their businesses run smoothly!

Carpet Cleaners

If your town is like mine, you see flyers from these guys all over town—and someone has to type them! This is a competitive business—and if you can help your client gain the biggest market share with your professional typing services, they will be eternally grateful!

Churches

Don't neglect your church when it comes time to market your typing services. From the weekly sermons to special programs and flyers, your church has many needs for typing—and you, as a church member, can fill those needs better than anyone else!

Consultants

You can find consultants in virtually every area of business. They are usually self-employed and during their busy times, they are in desperate need of efficient, professional typing help to keep it all together. Ask around or find these folks in your local Yellow Pages!

Construction Companies

If you live in an area where many houses or other buildings are being built, find out what construction companies are involved and inform them about your services. Busy construction companies make great clients for a home-based typist like you!

Dance Schools

If you live in a town of any size, there are probably many dance studios that offer instruction from children through adults. Typing needs can include class schedules, promotional flyers, records, and more!

Desktop Publishers

These individuals are often self-employed too, doing graphic design for a wide variety of clients. They often have the need for someone who can do fast, accurate data entry for large amounts of text that are used in creating brochures, books, reports, and more!

Entertainers

Even the smallest community has entertainers—from clowns to bands to local radio personalities. And these people have to promote themselves just like you do! With your typing service, you can help them create the flyers and correspondence they need for success!

Fund Raising Organizations

These organizations exist to help people raise money—a process that in-

volves lots of typing work for you! From lists of donors to plans for fund-raising events, you'll be an indispensable part of the team that makes it all happen.

Golf Courses

Golf clubs can be a real score for you as a home-based typist! They are always sponsoring special events that need special promotions—all of which involve the typing of invitations, programs, and more! Plus, there's membership typing to be considered as well.

Graphic Designers

Many graphic designers are home-based workers, and they are always coming up with projects that need to be typed! Whether it's a corporate brochure or annual report, or a program for the local arts center, all you need to remember is that graphic designers are artists, not typists!

Health Clubs

With the fitness craze at an all-time high, there are plenty of health clubs and fitness centers around that can use your typing services. From membership promotions to daily typing needs, this is a great place to market your services!

Immigration Consultants

If you live in or near a large city, check this out as a potential client base for you. You can bet these folks are busy and have the usual typing needs of any busy office. If you can speak, and type, in a language other than English, so much the better!

Kitchen Remodelers

Here's another field with lots of competition, especially in this day and age when so many people are remodeling their homes instead of buying new ones. Find a busy company that will keep you busy, too!

Landscape Contractors

While these talented individuals know about seeds and how to make things grow, they usually don't know much about typing! You can be the right-hand typist to a busy landscape contractor, and help him grow his business at the same time!

Limousine Services

Here's a business that really picks up at certain times of the year—and a smart limousine company goes all out with promotions at those times. As a reliable home-based typist, you can provide a much-needed service to this specialty business!

Mailing Services

These businesses exist to provide direct mailing services for businesses large and small. What that means to you, the home-based typist, is that there are endless mailing lists that need to be typed! This can be a steady, reliable client for you!

Martial Arts Studios

There's probably more than one martial arts studio near you, and just like everyone else, they have class schedules, promotional flyers, and other items that need to be typed. If you have an interest in martial arts, you'll be especially valuable to a client like this!

Massage Therapists

No longer just a part of life in California, massage therapists are now found all over the country. It's a competitive business, and they do all kinds of printed materials to promote themselves, including plenty of brochures and flyers—all of which need typing by someone like you!

Neighborhood Medical Clinics and Treatment Centers

There may be several walk-in medical clinics and specialized treatment centers in your community, and many more than that if you live in a large city. The doctors who work at these clinics may have the need for your typing services—and the medical center staff may need backup at busy times.

Nursing Homes

These facilities often have high turnover of their regular staff—which means you can have plenty of opportunities to fill in doing the typing of medical records and other vital information.

Opticians

Don't forget these friendly eye folks—they have many of the same typing needs as medical doctors.

Pet Hospitals

You guessed it—pets have medical records too! Everything that a regular doctor needs typed, a veterinarian will need typed as well. This can be a great opportunity if you love animals and want to be part of that working environment.

Photographers

Photographers and custom photo developers form a unique market that can be well worth your investigation. Their typing needs include business promotions, correspondence and maintaining current client lists and photo records.

Plumbers

You can't live without them, and they can't live without you! While they're off fixing sinks and drains, you can keep the typing back at the office from getting out of control. Try large plumbing firms that will need someone on-call to fill in for staff on occasion.

Printers

Here's a great idea that can really lead to some big work for you. Get to know one or more of the local printers in your community. Quick printers are great, but don't rule out larger printers as well. Leave your cards with the print reps and on bulletin boards, and you'll be sure to get calls for your typing services!

Private Schools

We've already talked about academic typing—but don't forget the private schools in your own home town that serve elementary, junior high, and high school-aged students! Teachers at these schools are often in need of typing services, and you might even be able to help the school's office staff out on occasion as well!

Property Management Services

This type of company handles the management of rental properties for a number of different owners. The bigger the company, the more work there is for a skilled professional typist like yourself!

Psychological Associations

These are organizations for professional psychologists. There is most likely a branch in your city. If you have any background in this area or have worked in the medical field, you may be able to get referrals from these and other professional medical associations.

Public Relations Firms

When the heat is on at public relations companies, they'll come running to you with piles of press releases and other juicy projects that need to be typed, pronto! This can be an especially good client for you because you'll learn things about public relations through working for them that you can apply to your own business!

Realtors

Realtors hand out more typed materials than just about anyone! With new properties constantly coming on the market, there's a constant need for property descriptions and flyers to be typed up. Not to mention correspondence and business documents—there's oodles of potential here!

Restaurants

How about typing menus for restaurants? This can be a great source of steady work, especially if you find restaurants that change their menus daily or weekly! If you can type very accurately and meet their tight deadlines, you'll have it made!

Resorts

If you live near a scenic area that attracts vacationers at a specific time of the year, you can be sure there are resorts who need your help! Whether it's the local ski lodge or hunting lodge, lakeshore inn or mountain hideaway, get to know these folks—they need plenty of typing!

Sports Schools

You'd be surprised at how many schools there are for specific sports—from baseball to tennis! Take a look in the Yellow Pages for the schools near you. You can bet that they need typing help for their advertising and promotions, not to mention record-keeping and day-to-day correspondence!

Swimming Pool Services

If you live in a warm climate where swimming pools abound, here's another great idea for finding loyal clients. Choose an enterprising individual or successful company, and help them become even more successful with your picture-perfect typing services!

Theaters

Who types all those programs for theater performances? You guessed it— someone just like you! If you've been bitten by the acting bug or just love hanging out around the theater, this type of client will be especially appealing to you. You might even be able to type scripts and other documents on occasion, too!

Translators

These individuals work on documents ranging in length from letters to book manuscripts. You may find very interesting typing work here, especially if you know more than one language. This can be especially good if you are part of a large foreign community located in a major U.S. city.

Travel Agencies

Travel agencies are always doing special promotions. They need flyers produced about everything from the latest Caribbean cruise to discounts in holiday airfares! Get to know a travel agency well, and they'll have your phone ringing off the hook!

Wedding Planners

Now here's a unique idea for new clients that's sure to be fun and exciting! Wedding planners are busy individuals who need to keep track of a multitude of details—and lists, lists, lists! You, as a professional typist, can offer your expert services to help get a wedding planner's business back on track!

Chapter 3:
Where to Get Training

If you are interested in how to make money typing, chances are you probably already know how to type. Even if you don't, however, it's just a matter of time before you, too, can be up and running with your own home typing business!

This chapter will talk about the kinds of skills you need, and where to obtain these skills if you don't have them already. You'll find it's a really a very simple matter to get started in this business. Compared to many other lines of work, the investment of time and money to start a home typing business is quite small. You can rest assured that the goal is within your reach!

So now, take a few moments to set your mind at ease by scanning the contents of this chapter. Then you'll be all set to follow the steps for setting up your own business that appear later on in the book.

Your Magic Fingers

The very first skill you need, of course, is the ability to type. A great many women (and a few brave men!) take typing class in high school. If that is where you learned to type, great! You probably have all the typing ability you need to start your own home business.

I learned how to type when I was a senior in high school, mainly because my mother thought it would be a good skill to have. I really didn't plan on being a secretary for the rest of my life, but somehow I felt my mother was probably right—and sure enough, she was! I've only once worked as a secretary in an office, but my typing skills have been invaluable to me over the years.

Now I wasn't the best typist in my high school class—I remember one girl in particular who was a real whiz at the keyboard—but I wasn't the worst, either. Before too long I got my speed up to 65 words a minute. Then I got a job typing for the local newspaper in my home town—and the typing class wasn't even over yet! Was I ever thrilled!

I continued to work as a typist for various book and magazine publishers. When I was in my mid-twenties, newly divorced and out of work, I decided to start my own typing service. I put an ad in the local paper and was amazed by the response! I got three regular clients from that tiny ad: one was a real estate agent, one was a husband-and-wife massage team, and one was a famous author. The real estate agent needed letters and contracts typed; the massage team needed brochures and flyers typed up; and the famous author wrote the first draft of all his books by talking them into a tape recorder. Someone had to transcribe the tapes, and it turned out that someone was me!

So, there you have it—one person's story of starting a home typing business with nothing more than a high school typing class! If you have high school typing under your belt, all you have to do is get your fingers limbered up and you'll be ready to go! Should you feel the need for some extra help, just run down to your local bookstore and see what books they have on typing. Brush up by completing a few lessons in one of those books, and it will bring your self-confidence (<u>and</u> your typing!) up to speed.

What If You Don't Type?

If you don't type at all, or if your typing skills are very minimal, you might want to enroll in a class. In many communities you can find FREE classes in typing through a community college or an adult education program. For example, in my community you can take free classes in beginning keyboarding or brush-up instruction in typing.

So, first I suggest that you contact your local community college or adult education program and ask about classes in typing. The price is right, and you can sometimes arrange with the instructor to complete these classes at your own pace, and on your own schedule. For people with families or other obligations, this can be a real life saver!

What About Business Schools?

Business schools are another good place to learn typing and other office skills. Of course, they <u>will</u> cost you some money. Exactly how much varies from school to school. But the right business school can be well worth the investment.

Just to give you an idea of the commitment involved, one business school in my town offers three to nine month programs in legal, medical, business, and secretarial skills. You have your choice of taking the classes one at a time, or enrolling full-time in the whole program. They not only teach typing and word processing, but they also have a class called "Computerized Keyboarding." Now that kind of class could be very good for you if you have or plan to buy a computer!

There are literally hundreds of business schools across the nation. To locate the business schools in your state, go to your local library reference desk and ask to see a copy of the *American Trade Schools Directory*. This directory is published every year. All you have to do is look under your state, then under the headings "Business" and "Secretarial." The names, addresses, and phone numbers of all the schools offering business classes are right there!

Call the schools nearest you and ask them to send you a list of the classes they offer. If they have an official catalog, ask them to send you a copy. Here are some additional points to keep in mind when you talk to business schools:

• Is the school accredited? For your own protection, make sure the school has accreditation from an appropriate state or national organization.

• Does the school have an admission exam and screening process? These two items are important because they allow both you and the school to see if you're the right "fit." And if the school is not right for you, you'll know right away!

• Does the school offer a placement program? A good business school will offer you job placement services after you've completed your courses. Some schools offer lifetime placement services!

• Does the school offer the classes you need? Beware of schools that teach outdated subjects like shorthand (a skill that's been replaced just about everywhere by the Dictaphone). Concentrate on developing your word processing and computer skills to start, then add the Dictaphone and other office skills later.

• What about equipment? Make sure the school has up-to-date equipment. If at all possible, learn your typing skills on a word processor or computer. At this point in time, electric typewriters are practically a thing of the past—you could almost say they've gone the way of the dinosaur!

Transcription

Transcription is another skill that you're likely to need in your home typing business. Simply stated, transcription is the ability to type words that are spoken onto a tape recorder. These days, busy executives are in the habit of keeping tape recorders in their car and on their desk. Often they use tiny tape recorders with miniature tapes called "microcassettes." They dictate letters, reports, etc. right onto the tape, which you then transcribe and turn into professional-looking documents.

There are many different kinds of transcription equipment available. When I transcribed tapes for the writer I talked about earlier in this chapter, I used a simple foot pedal I bought at Radio Shack for less than $10. This pedal plugged into the back of my tape recorder and allowed me to advance and rewind the tape as I did my typing.

Of course, you can get much more sophisticated transcription equipment. The kind generally used in offices today is commonly called a Dictaphone. It has a foot pedal attached to a tape machine, plus headphones. You listen to the tape through the headphones, using the built-in foot pedal to advance and rewind the tape at will.

Becoming a good transcriptionist is really just a matter of practice. You can take a class in it, but there's no reason you can't learn by doing. It can sometimes be tricky to distinguish another person's words when they're spoken onto a tape; when the tape is garbled or the words seem to run together, you just make your best guess and type a question mark beside it so your client will take a second look.

My advice is to hold off on investing in expensive transcription equipment until you are absolutely positive that transcription will be a big part of your business. But I do recommend adding transcription to the list of services you offer. Good transcriptionists are hard to come by, and this can be a very profitable part of your business, especially if you can get into legal or medical transcription (see Chapters 4 and 5 for more details).

The Story of Kathy Z.

Kathy Z. is a home-based typist that specializes in transcription work. When she started her business, she didn't have any special training. She just started typing on the side, and then bought a computer and taught herself how to use it. As she tells it, "I had done some word processing but I didn't know anything about computers. I went to the computer store and said, 'Tell me, what should I get?'"

Now Kathy has an IBM-compatible 386 computer. The software programs she uses the most are WordPerfect 5.0 and 5.1. She has a very good transcribing machine too, and she says that these days similar machines cost between $250 and $500.

Kathy says that 80% of her work involves tape transcriptions. She says, "I have specialized in doing reports from the vocational rehabilitation field, because I got a reputation in this area. I also have one or two lawyers and I do a lot of resumes."

She got her first big client from a newspaper ad—the company was looking for a typist, and they were happy to hire someone working freelance out of their home. (As you can imagine, Kathy's advice to those just starting out is "Read the want ads!") Kathy charges $25 an hour. She suggests not quoting page rates, saying, "If the text is clear, the client will benefit and if it is difficult to read, I don't lose."

The Typing Addiction

According to Kathy, "Typing is like an addiction. My adrenaline kicks in and I can keep going for hours and hours and hours. I like typing because I meet different people and learn about a lot of different things. It's better than working as a typist in some sort of office, like real estate, where you generate the same kinds of documents all day. When you have a variety of clients, the work is never boring.

Although there are plenty of good typing services in town, Kathy sets herself apart by giving extra good quality service. She says, "I make suggestions, point out mistakes, and make corrections. I always work closely with my clients. In my experience, typing is a service industry built on personal relationships. Some of my clients say I should have a counseling service in addition to a typing service!"

Ten-Key Calculators and Spreadsheets

For certain types of clients, you might find it useful to be proficient on a ten-key calculator—or to know computer programs that do spreadsheets, like Excel or Lotus. If you think you might need these skills, by all means take a class at your local community college or adult education center to get you up to speed.

Computer programs like Excel and Lotus allow you to create customized charts, worksheets, spreadsheets, and databases. One example of a great way to use these programs is to maintain mailing lists for your clients. You start by entering all the names for the mailing list in a database, which you can then use to print out labels on your computer printer. This is an important job for many clients—and if you can keep their mailing list updated and print out labels whenever they want, you'll soon prove yourself to be indispensable to them!

Your Best Assets: Speed and Accuracy

By all means, I recommend that you practice your typing skills to improve your speed and accuracy. The faster you are, the more you'll impress your clients—and the more money you can charge for your services!

Mary T., a full-time, home-based typist who has her office out in the garage, told me the story of how she built her business. Just like me, all she had when she started was basic typing skills from high school. Unlike me, however, she could type 110 words a minute!

After Mary had worked as an executive secretary for several bosses, she decided that she was tired of working for somebody else. So, she took the plunge and started her own business by placing a simple ad in the local newspaper that said "Typing 110 WPM" and her phone number.

Lo and behold, Mary got several big clients from her ad, and she was off and running. Those first clients were general contractors and structural engineers who needed specification sheets typed. That's now the area that Mary specializes in, since her clients have been so happy with her work that they've referred others in the field to her.

Mary charges $25 an hour for her services—and because she is so fast and accurate, she could probably charge even more if she wanted to. But she likes her business the way it is. She says, "I might see some clients only two or three times a year, but they consistently return to me and they also tell their friends."

Mary's Equipment Tips

Mary uses an IBM Displaywriter for her business, which is a dedicated word processor. (See the description of a dedicated word processor in Chapter 11). She plans to buy a computer soon and stick with IBM. Here's her advice on equipment: "Be sure you have a good service contract. Along with a good product, you need to have a good repairman who knows your machine and will be there within a half hour when you call—because when your equipment is down, no work is possible!"

The Downtown Blues

For a short time, Mary had an office downtown. She much prefers working at home, and I thought you'd like to hear her reasons why:

"I like working at home a lot better than working out of an office downtown because it's freed me. When I was downtown, I wasted a lot of time waiting for clients. At home, clients seldom drop in without calling ahead. Often they just put something in the mail. If I do have to pick up work in the evenings or on weekends, I just go downstairs instead of driving downtown, hunting for a parking space, and waiting.

"There's nothing I can't do here that I did downtown. I like freelance typing. I didn't want to make a commitment to a large organization and with kids, my time is my own. I can take summers off. There is a nice variety and nice hours. I can work when the kids are in school, and I'm home when my son comes home for lunch.

"The trend is to work at home. Everyone should. It's neat. You can have a life outside your machine, and I can take time off and not worry about it. With phone, fax, and overnight couriers, why not work out of your home? You don't have to hassle with parking and overhead—and that's not just rent but also things like business improvement taxes, parking taxes, business organization taxes, etc."

Building a Niche

You might have noticed from the stories of Kathy and Mary in this chapter that they both had a "niche"—a certain kind of work that they were known for. Kathy specializes in reports for the vocational rehabilitation field, and Mary specializes in specification sheets for general contractors and structural engineers.

Another thing you might have noticed is that these two women developed their niches naturally from the first clients they got as freelance typists. They did a good job and got referrals to other people in the same field by word of mouth. This is the most painless way to grow your business.

Here's a summary of strategies to keep in mind for building your very own niche:

- **Read the newspaper for want ads for typists.**
- **Run your own ad to advertise your typing services.**

- Do a fast and accurate job for all of your clients.

- Watch the referrals come pouring in!

What About Carpal Wrist Syndrome?

With all the hoopla lately about carpal wrist syndrome (also known as carpal tunnel syndrome), should you be worried? This condition is a repetitive-motion disorder that afflicts people who move their bodies in the same way over and over for extended periods of time. In recent years typists seem to have been afflicted with it in droves. People in other occupations, such as musicians, can develop it as well.

Carpal wrist syndrome is indeed very painful and sometimes must be treated with surgery. However, here is an amazing fact: of all the home-based typists I spoke to while researching this book, <u>not a single one had ever experienced it!</u>

My theory is that home-based typists have many advantages over typists working in an office situation—and that these advantages lead to the prevention of carpal wrist syndrome. Working at home, you are free to get up and move around as often as you like, with no one looking over your shoulder. You're never chained to your keyboard, and you have more variety in your work than a typist working at the same office day in and day out.

Perhaps most important of all is that, without exception, the home-based typists whose stories are in this book love their work! How many people holding down a dull office job can say that? I believe that boredom and unhappiness are factors just as important to the development of carpal wrist syndrome as repetitive motion.

If you want to take special precautions against this disorder, you can buy a special adjustable keyboard that splits into two parts down the middle. By changing the angle of the keyboard, you can change the position of your hands slightly and eliminate the repetitive motion.

Another good idea is a "wrist rest" that sits in front of your keyboard. When you pause for a few seconds, your wrists naturally fall onto the padded wrist rest, instead of just staying suspended in the air. Wrist rests cost around $10 in stationery stores.

Take On The World!

This chapter has provided you with all the basic information you need to get your typing skills up to speed—plus stories of actual typists to show you how it can be done! Use this chapter as a guide to locating the training you need, if any—and know that soon you'll be the happy owner of your own home-based typing service!

Chapter 4: Resumes

Resumes can be an important part of your home-based typing business. There is so much work available preparing resumes that you might even choose to make it the focus of your business!

Kim Marino in Santa Barbara, California did just that. She devoted her entire business to writing and designing resumes for people. She called her business "Just Resumes." Then she went on to write several books on the subject.

Kim's books are excellent guides to the preparation of highly effective resumes. Using her techniques, you can offer a resume-writing service that's a cut above the ordinary. Instead of just typing up the resume someone hands to you, you can offer suggestions on how to make it more effective so they really get the job they're after!

This chapter will talk about the requirements of resumes and how you can build this skill into a healthy profit center for your home-based business!

Books About Resumes

Kim Marino's books on resume writing are very useful for newcomers to the field. They are *The College Student's Resume Guide* and *The Resume Guide for Women of the '90s*. (Both are published by Ten Speed Press.)

Take a look at these and other books about resumes to learn about requirements for formatting. Resumes are specialized documents. They have a job to do: to get your client a job! And as you will soon learn, the key to success is to design a specific resume for a specific job. That's why you, as a resume expert, can offer a service to your potential clients that they just can't get anywhere else.

The Psychology of Resumes

People who need resumes are often in a panic. They just saw an ad in the newspaper for a job they want, or they just heard about a new opening through a friend of theirs, or they just lost their job unexpectedly—and all of a sudden they realize that they need a resume. Their old resume might be years out of date, or in some cases, they might never have had a resume before. They need your help!

Oftentimes these people will bring you some scribbles on scraps of paper. They might have tried to type up the resume themselves and realized it was hopeless. They might not even be sure what to say at all. By the time they call you, they need a resume so badly that they will be only too happy to pay you top dollar for your professional advice on resume design and your word processing expertise!

Your job is to take whatever background information your clients give you and transform it into a thing of beauty! There's no doubt about it, a professional-looking resume can make or break a person's chances of getting the job they want. So here are some resume basics that will help you produce exceptional resumes every time!

What to Charge

For basic word processing of resumes, the going rate is $25-$40 per page. But if you help write and design the resume, you can charge much more. Kim, the expert we talk about in this chapter, charges $100 for writing, designing, and typing a one-page resume. Then she charges $25 per quarter page for the second page. That means if the resume turns out to be a page and a half long, she charges $150.

Kim figures it takes her two hours to write, design and type the first page. So that means she is making $50 an hour. Now that's an hourly wage you can live with, I'm sure! Read on to learn about resume basics and how to get started with this very profitable career!

Resume Basics

• The ideal length of a resume is one page. Whenever possible, try to arrange the information so it fits comfortably on a single piece of paper. You need to have adequate margins around all sides so it doesn't look too crowded. The standard is to have 1 inch margins on each side, and 1/2 inch margins on the top and the bottom. If the information won't fit into this format, go to a second page.

• Use bold type and underlining for the information you want a potential employer to notice in the first few seconds. Most employers take only 30 seconds or so to scan a resume. In that brief amount of time, a decision is made to put the resume in the "yes" pile or the circular file. So you must make sure the resume will get their attention right away!

• The type size should not be smaller than 11 point. The type style should be sensible and professional. Don't get too fancy with decorative or unusual typefaces; they distract the employer from the information at hand.

• Recommend that your clients use ordinary paper like plain white or off-white to make copies of their resume. For a special touch they can choose a paper with a linen or "laid" texture, which always looks very professional. Many people make the mistake of using a bright color or an unusual textured paper that they think will make their resume stand out. Such tactics will get them attention all right, but definitely not the kind of attention they want!

The Two Types of Resumes

There are two main classifications of resumes. The first is the chronological resume. This is the kind of resume that is probably the most familiar to you. It lists the person's entire work experience in order by date, starting with the person's most recent job and working backwards. The chronological resume is perfect for people who have a stable work history, who have always worked in the same field, and who have a different job description for each job they have held.

The second kind of resume is known as a functional resume. This resume format is perfect for people who want to highlight particular skills. If the person has a checkered work history with a wide variety of skills and jobs, you only pick the jobs that are the most relevant to the position the person wants. Then you organize them under headings for each skill. Functional resumes also work very well for people who have big gaps in their work history—and even people who have never worked before!

Resume Checklist

Every resume needs to include an appropriate combination of the following items. As a resume writing professional, you will be able to help each client decide what would be best for him or her.

• Name, Address, and Telephone Number. This is pretty much self-explanatory. It's the first thing to go on the resume, at the very top. Usually this information is centered and the name is typed in all caps.

• Employment Objective. This lets the employer know right away what kind of job the person is after.

• Professional Profile. This lists a brief summary of the talents a person can bring to the job. Usually each item starts with a bullet point and is no more than one or two lines long.

• Professional Experience. This gives a detailed description of the person's skills, without naming specific jobs the person has held.

• Education. All education that is relevant to the position at hand is listed here. Include college degrees, professional training certificates, internships, seminars, continuing education, etc. Do not list high school.

• Employment history. This section can be prominent if the person's employment history is impressive. If the person has little or no employment history, this section can be designed to highlight volunteer work or any other unpaid work that the person has done over the years.

What About Personal Data?

In the past resumes used to include a lot of personal information—things like hobbies, birth date, height, weight, marital status, etc. As a general rule, personal data is not appropriate for resumes in this day and age. Why?

Well, affirmative action, for one thing. By law, employers are not allowed to discriminate on the basis of age, sex, marital status, or anything else. So there is no reason to provide them with that information in a resume. You can do your clients a service by explaining this to them.

Be Choosy About What to Include

Some people want to put everything they have ever done onto their resume. This is not always the best idea. By and large, employers will only care about work history that relates specifically to what the person can do for them. As a professional resume preparer, you can help separate the wheat from the chaff.

For example, Kim tells a story of a client who wanted to find work as a medical therapist. He had recently changed fields from years of being a salesman and gone to school for two years to learn his new profession. His resume listed all his experience as a salesman, and he found himself unable to get a job as a medical therapist. Kim redesigned his resume to include ONLY information about his medical training, including internships. That did the trick, and he got the job he wanted!

You can help your clients who need resumes put their best foot forward. Design each resume so the person looks perfect for the specific job they have in mind. Take the best of what they have in terms of education and background, and highlight that information in every way you can. Give the employer what they are looking for, and the person will get the job!

Electronic Resumes

Electronic resumes are becoming common in some industries, especially high-tech industries. These are resumes that are sent to prospective employers via fax modem or electronic mail. If you have a fax modem or e-mail capabilities for your business anyway, it will be easy for you to add electronic resumes to your list of services.

You can design an electronic resume in the same way you do a regular resume, but don't use any bold or underlining. Also, there should be certain "buzz words" on these types of resumes. The best thing to do is to look at some examples to get an idea of what's hot and what's not.

Kim's Resume Preparation Strategy

Over the years Kim has developed a unique resume preparation strategy. She sits down with her clients and creates the resume on the spot. The entire process takes two hours for a one-page resume.

She starts out by interviewing the client right in her office. First she asks about their job objective, and then she asks additional questions to find out what information will enhance that objective. The client leaves her office with a completed resume, ready to go!

Kim says, "It took me awhile to perfect this method, but it is the most efficient use of my time." You can see why: clients don't have to come back to get mistakes corrected, and they can read and approve the work right away. When the job is done, it's done for good—though you always need to keep a copy on disk in case the client needs it updated later, or needs revisions to make the resume appropriate to a new job search!

Equipment

You can use just about any word processing equipment to produce top quality resumes. Since the appearance of the finished product is so important, be sure you have a decent printer. For resumes, your printer is almost more important than what kind of computer you have! A laser printer is ideal, though an ink jet printer may be acceptable in some cases. A word to the wise: dot matrix printers are definitely not acceptable for producing final copies of resumes!

For software, use a basic word processing program like Word Perfect or Microsoft Word. There's no need to use desktop publishing software for resumes, since they usually do not have photographs or illustrations of any kind. Speaking of which, that brings us to the topic of . . .

Photographs and Illustrations

Generally speaking, photographs and illustrations are not appropriate for use on a resume. People like actors/actresses and models will always include a big 8 x 10 glossy photo with their resume anyway. That is definitely the way to go for people who work in fields where physical appearance is everything.

Keep the resume "plain vanilla" and let the information do the talking. Remember that employers are bound by anti-discrimination laws and will not appreciate all the trouble you took to put a photograph on a resume. Above all else, it's most important for your client to be perceived as a professional. Make sure the resume you provide will do just that—no more and no less!

The Cover Letter

Every resume that your client sends out needs a cover letter to go with it. Here's another potential money-maker for you! Explain to your clients that you can write and type their cover letters as well as their resumes, and you will tap into yet another great source of income. Because a cover letter highlights the client's skills, which you have already covered in the resume, you are the perfect person to do the job. A good cover letter with a professional-looking resume is a winning combination for your clients!

How To Find Clients

If you live in a college town, you have a huge built-in market at your fingertips. College students always need resumes. It can be a very good idea to advertise in the college newspaper. Classified ads in these newspapers cost very little. You can also put up signs around campus. Once you do a few resumes, word of mouth will kick in as students pass the word along.

Another great way to break in is advertising in the Yellow Pages. While it will cost you some money up front, that money works for you all year long as frantic people let their fingers do the walking right to your resume preparation service! This is how Kim Marino got her first clients, and it can work just as well for you, too!

There are the other tried and true methods for getting work: advertising in your local newspaper, putting up fliers around town, and passing out your business cards. Another idea is to team up with an employment agency. Tell them about your services and get them to put you on a referral list for people to call if they need a resume.

Job Security—For You!

One thing about producing resumes for people is that you yourself will always have job security! There will always be people who need resumes. Plus you get the satisfaction of helping someone who really needs your services. People will be grateful for your assistance at the crucial time in their lives when they are applying for a new job. If you like working with people, you're sure to find that the daily rewards of resume preparation are great—both personally and financially!

Sample Chronological Resume

MARY J. JOHNSON, C.P.A.

111 Park Lane
Anytown, USA 11223
xxx-xxx-xxxx

Objective: Staff Accounting position to use my skills and abilities.

EDUCATION	Big City University, Summer 1990 TA 318 Federal Income Taxation for Individuals
	BS Degree, Business Administration, 1985 Big City University, Big City, USA Concentration: Accounting
	AS Degree, Business Economics, 1980 Big City University, Big City, USA
PROFESSIONAL ORGANIZATIONS	American Institute of Certified Public Accountants Arizona Society of Certified Public Accountants

PROFESSIONAL EXPERIENCE

1986-present

SMITH & SMITH, Big City, USA
Staff Accountant
• Prepared various types of complex tax returns.
• Examined compilations, reviews and audits.
• Acted as a client service representative.
• Developed technical knowledge in various areas of taxation and accounting.
• Supervised staff members.

1985-86

JOHN Q. JONES, C.P.A., Big City, USA
Accounting Assistant
• Prepared accounts receivable and payable, monthly billing statements and payroll.
• Assisted accountants in the preparation of financial statements for various clients.
• Developed knowledge of computers.

1983-84

BIG SCIENCE CORPORATION, Big City, USA
Cost Accounting Assistant
• Assisted product line controller in preparing reports
• Generated reports for annual audit.

REFERENCES AVAILABLE UPON REQUEST

Sample Functional Resume

LOUISE A. SMITH

1200 Main St.
Anytown, USA 11223
xxx-xxx-xxxx

Objective: Bookkeeping position

EDUCATION

Business Administration, 1988-89
Anytown Community College, Anytown, USA

Any State Teaching Credential, 1983
Any State University, Big City, USA

BS Degree, Education, 1969
Out of State University, Any State, USA

OFFICE SKILLS

Accounts receivable . . . accounts payable . . . general ledgers and journals . . . payroll . . . bank reconciliation . . . balance sheets . . . computer skills . . . Microsoft Word and Word Perfect word processing . . . excellent phone, customer and employee relations skills . . . typing 65 wpm . . . ten key touch.

PROFESSIONAL EXPERIENCE

Management & Bookkeeping
• Assisted in establishing a structure for a growing company.
 – Set up and maintained bookkeeping procedures for accounts receivable, payable and general ledgers.
• In charge of managing three very service-oriented Sizzler Restaurants.
 – Prepared detailed labor cost and analysis, weekly statistical reports and analyzed annual profit and loss statements.
 – Conducted monthly motivational and educational staff meetings.
 – Performed weekly accounting procedures for accounts receivable, payable and inventory control.
 – Hired, trained and supervised 40 employees at each location.

EMPLOYMENT HISTORY

Home Management, Travel, Studies	1984-present
6-7 Grade Teacher, Any Town School District, Any Town, USA	1979-83
Manager, Sizzler Corporation, Any City, USA	1977-79
Bookkeeper, Any State Gas Company, Any City, USA	Summers 1965-75

Sample Cover Letter

MARY J. JOHNSON, C.P.A.

111 Park Lane
Anytown, USA 11223
xxx-xxx-xxxx

April 20, 1995

Brian Harris, Regional Manager
XYZ Corporation
PO Box 1000
Any City, USA 11223

Dear Mr. Harris:

I am interested in applying for an accounting position and understand that your company is currently recruiting qualified employees with these skills.

I offer 12 years experience in the accounting field. With my background in preparing complex tax returns and my superior skills in client service, I am confident that I can make an important contribution to your company now, and in the years to come.

Enclosed is my resume which provides additional information about my education and experience. I would appreciate the opportunity to meet with you to discuss how my qualifications would be consistent with your needs.

Sincerely,

(signature here)

Mary J. Johnson

Enclosure: Resume

Chapter 5:
Medical Typing

Medical typing is one of the most profitable areas you can choose for your home typing business. It is a specialized field, and it can require some specialized medical background—but this knowledge is easily gained. You might even have the know-how already if you have ever worked for a hospital or a doctor.

There are two distinct kinds of medical typing. One is medical secretary work, which includes compiling medical records, charts, and correspondence. Just about any home-based typist can do this kind of medical typing work, since it does not require too much medical background.

I talked to one home-based typist who did general medical typing, and she had no previous experience working in a hospital. So, while some experience working in a hospital setting may be to your advantage, it's not absolutely necessary to break in. Speed and accuracy, of course, are the most important attributes you can bring to this type of work! Once the hospitals and doctors know you and the quality of your work, you'll have more than enough to keep you busy.

The other kind of medical typing is medical transcription work, which requires more specialized medical knowledge and a Dictaphone—but has great financial rewards for you. This chapter will focus on medical transcription work, explaining the ins and outs of this fascinating field!

What is Medical Transcription?

Have you ever looked at a prescription scribbled in your doctor's handwriting, and wondered how anyone could understand what it meant? Well, medical transcription is kind of like that—it's somewhat like a foreign language, and as such, it takes a little bit of time to learn.

A medical transcriptionist needs to be familiar with medical terminology. This includes the parts of the body, the names of surgical instruments, X ray and surgical procedures, and the names of drugs and other knowledge of pharmacology. Some transcribers specialize in a particular field, such as psychiatry, pathology, or osteology.

You can take courses at business colleges in medical transcription. (See the information on finding business colleges in Chapter 3.) There are also practice tapes and even internship programs available on the subject. And of course, there's no substitute for actually working in a hospital for a year or two. Just being around the language of medicine every day will help you progress that much faster.

It's a Matter of Life and Death!

Medical transcription is literally a life and death field. The doctors trust you and don't always check everything. When it's late at night in the emergency room, doctors may not pick up on a typing error and they may do the wrong thing. So you really need to know medical terminology in order to be a good medical transcriptionist!

Just as an example, here are three words that sound more or less the same but have very different meanings: perineal (crouch area); peroneal (a nerve); and peritoneal (lining inside the stomach). You get the idea. As a transcriptionist, all you have to work from are cassette tapes made by the doctors. You need to train your ear to pick up on the subtle differences between these words. It takes some time, but believe me, it's worth the effort!

How Much Can You Make?

I spoke to one woman, Mona, who owns a small medical transcription business that employs home-based workers. She says, "My company rewards high productivity. My best typists worked for hospitals or offices where they more than pulled their own weight. My workers typically make between $20,000-$40,000 a year for full time work. I have one employee who makes $90,000, but she is very fast."

Well, as you can see, the sky is pretty much the limit for medical transcription work! How would you feel about making $90,000 a year? Would that be worth investing some time in learning the ins and outs of the medical transcription field? I'm willing to bet that you might think so!

What Equipment Do You Need?

Most medical transcribers work from tapes that doctors walk around with and talk into. Doctors have been known to use their recorders virtually any time and any place—one typist I talked to said that she knew a doctor who dictated during Mass at church!

To do the work right, you'll need a standard DOS-based computer (an IBM or compatible), a computer printer, the usual office equipment, and a Dictaphone. Rest assured that you'll be in good company working from home as a medical transcriptionist. In my city of 100,000 people, there is only one medical transcriptionist that works out of an office—all of the rest of them work out of their homes!

Your Clients: Hospitals and Doctors

As a medical transcriptionist, you will get work from hospitals and from doctors, both in group practice and private practice. Hospitals need good medical transcribers to ensure accurate record keeping. Hospitals can actually lose their accreditation if their records are not accurate!

For private doctors, transcribed records are necessary if their patients go to the hospital. Their own scribbles on a chart just won't do—the records must be typed so they can be understood by all hospital personnel.

When they are admitted to a hospital, patients need a history and a physical report. If there is surgery, there is an operation report. If rehabilitation is prescribed, yet another report is needed. Pathology tests and discharges also require reports. When doctors fax records, they have to be in typed form. And who is going to do all this typing? Medical transcribers like yourself, of course!

The Insurance Snafu

Insurance companies will use any excuse not to pay claims—and poor records is one of those excuses. If medical records are not legible—meaning, if they are not typed properly—the insurance companies may deny coverage. So you can see why hospitals and doctors, as well as patients, can't live without medical transcriptionists!

Confidentiality

Perhaps more than any other area of home-based typing, confidentiality is of the utmost importance when you are dealing with medical transcription. This even extends to not leaving cassette tapes out on your front porch or in your mailbox for pickup or delivery. The doctors or hospitals you work for will be liable if patient confidentiality is broken. A doctor may have his or her license revoked if information about a patient is divulged without that patient's authorization.

Some clients may want you to do work electronically, via modem and fax. If this is the case, be sure that you use a private phone line at all times—do not go through the Internet, where confidentiality cannot be controlled. You may pay more in phone charges, but it is the only ethical way to go. Your clients will understand and appreciate the need for phone lines to be secure at all times.

It goes without saying that the rule of confidentiality applies to you yourself as well. You must never repeat anything you read or type about a patient. Also, never repeat information about a patient's illness to your friends or family, even if you do not mention the patient's name.

In this same vein, it's important not to leave medical papers lying around on your desk when you leave the room. Keep your papers neat and file them in a locked drawer if you can at the end of the day. While this measure may seem excessive, just remember that it would take only one incident of broken confidentiality to ruin the trust your clients have placed in you! So play it safe, and take extra precautions at all times in word, thought, and deed to maintain confidentiality.

Basic Office Accessories

As a medical transcriptionist, there are a few office accessories that you really can't live without. A good English dictionary and a good medical dictionary are a must. Another reference book called the *Physician's Desk Reference* will be very helpful to you. Also, invest in a good secretarial handbook that can be a guide to grammar and word usage.

Charlotte's Story

Charlotte, a successful medical transcriptionist, had this to say about herself and her work:

"I wanted to be a surgeon. I had a lot of premed courses, got married, got divorced, and had to go to work. For medical transcribing, medical background is very important. Many typists start working in hospitals to get training and then strike out on their own.

"I have a saying: I'll do the transcriptions, let the doctors save lives. If the doctors make mistakes, I correct them. It's second nature. I want them to have a report that they are proud of. I clean up stuff all the time. I'll flag the report if I see a medical inconsistency—for example, if the report says the patient is allergic to penicillin and that the patient has been started on an antibiotic that has a penicillin base. I'm a partner with the doctors."

Charlotte's attitude about being a partner with the doctors has made her one of the most successful medical transcriptionists in her area. This is an attitude you will definitely want to adopt as you carve out a niche for yourself in this exciting field.

New Products: Less Bang For Your Buck

Because medical transcription is a "big buck" field, there are lots of vendors offering new products. One is a digital dictation system that takes transcriptions over the phone line. This system allows doctors to phone in a report which instantly gets converted into a computer file. Then a printed report can be returned to the client via modem.

These digital dictation systems are very expensive—some can cost up to $250,000!—so they are obviously not for home-based medical transcriptionists. But doctors aren't used to using this approach anyway. They would rather talk into a tape recorder and hand you the tape.

In a variation on this theme, one home-based medical transcriptionist said that she installed a dedicated phone line in her office which had a tape recorder, so doctors could call in their transcriptions over the phone. But not one of her doctor clients used it! It just goes to show that technology isn't everything it's cracked up to be—and that old habits die hard.

Another "hot" new product is voice recognition systems. While they're the latest thing on the market, the transcriptionists I talked to say that the technology is still at least five to ten years off. The machines that are on the market now are not worth the investment for the home-based medical transcriptionist. First of all, in order for the machine to work, the doctor has to speak very slowly—which doctors just don't do, since they are very busy people and always in a hurry! Second, the machines readily confuse terms, which can be dangerous for medical records.

So whatever you do, don't invest your hard-earned money in a voice recognition machine—the companies who make them will not let you lease the equipment or get your money back!

Getting Your First Client

With all those doctors and hospitals out there just waiting for your services, it's more a question of where to begin than how to begin!

The easiest way to break into the field is to have worked in a hospital or for a doctor prior to starting your own medical transcription business. If this is the case, let your former department head and any staff members you like know that you're going out on your own and you'd be more than happy to help with any overload work they might have. Since you know their routine and policies already, you're the most logical person for them to choose for extra typing jobs!

You might send a letter like the one on the next page to all the staff doctors at the hospital. You can use the same approach even if you have not worked in a hospital before. All of your potential customers are listed in the local phone book. Contact each potential doctor and hospital one by one, and you are sure to break in.

Here are some other ideas:

• Write a notice for hospital bulletin boards and get permission to post it on every bulletin board you can find!

• Write a short press release which states who you are, what you have to offer, and how you can be contacted. Send this press release to all the local newspapers. (See sample press release on page 66.)

• Scan your local paper for notices of new medical practices starting up. Call or send a letter to let them know about your service. (See page 65.)

To Sum Up

Medical transcription is a big business, and it is getting bigger. This field is so lucrative because of all the paperwork generated by hospitals and doctors. You can be sure this amount of paperwork is not going to lessen. If anything, it is bound to increase—meaning only more work for medical transcriptionists like yourself!

So, while this branch of home typing has its own special demands, the rewards are well worth the effort you'll put in up front. If you learn something about the medical field and apply yourself to the task, your services will be sought after by the medical community in your area—and you'll have the satisfaction of knowing that you're making a valuable contribution to the health and well being of a great many people. Now, what could be better than that?

Sample Letter

Today's Date

Dr. William Jones
Big City Hospital
100 Main Street
Big City, USA 11111

Dear Dr. Jones:

After working as a medical transcriber at Big City Hospital, I've decided to take a big step forward and open my own medical transcribing service.

While it's always difficult to leave a familiar job, I hope that we can still be in touch. I'm enclosing a few of my business cards, so you can contact me if you would like to use my service.

Please feel free to call 24 hours a day at xxx-xxxx. My regular office hours are from 8 am to 5 pm, but my answering machine is on at all hours. I also pick up and deliver and offer one-day turnaround on rush jobs.

Thanks for your time, and I look forward to working with you!

Sincerely,

(signature)

Candy Baker
Candy's Medical Transcribing Service
333 Harmony Lane
Sweet Suburb, USA 22222

Sample Press Release

Today's Date

FOR IMMEDIATE RELEASE

Contact:
Candy Baker
Candy's Medical Transcribing Service
333 Harmony Lane
Sweet Suburb, USA 22222
xxx-xxx-xxxx

BAKER OPENS MEDICAL TRANSCRIBING SERVICE

Any Town, USA—Candy Baker announces that she has opened Candy's Medical Transcribing Service, specializing in medical word processing and transcription.

A long-time resident of Any Town, Baker has worked as a medical transcriber at Big City Hospital. The new business offers free pickup and delivery service to all doctors in Any Town. For more information, call Candy's Medical Transcribing Service at xxx-xxxx.

###

For more information, contact Candy's Medical Transcribing Service, 333 Harmony Lane, Sweet Suburb, USA 22222; xxx-xxx-xxxx.

Chapter 6:
Legal Typing

Like medical typing, legal typing means big money for you. The home-based legal typists and transcriptionists we talked to make $25 an hour! And the good news is, it's easy to make the transition from general word processing to legal word processing. All you need is a good working knowledge of your equipment and an understanding of how to format legal documents.

While the legal field has plenty of specialized terminology, you can still format legal documents without having to understand every word you type. As time goes on, you <u>will</u> begin to understand more and more legal terms, and that will make you even more valuable to your lawyer clients!

This chapter explains the ins and outs of legal transcription to help you get started in this very profitable field. There are more lawyers and more cases being tried right now than at any other time in the history of this country! Make no mistake about it, law is big business—and you reap the rewards yourself when you become a home-based legal transcriptionist.

How to Get Legal Experience

The very best way to become familiar with legal word processing and transcription is to work in a law office. Nancy T., a home-based legal transcriptionist, had no experience whatsoever when she first started out in the legal field. She was just a good typist who had taken typing classes in high school. Just by chance, Nancy was offered the opportunity to work in a lawyer's office answering the phones and doing word processing—in exchange for her rent! She then proceeded to learn everything she needed to know about the legal field while she was on the job.

Nancy says, "Attorneys will often teach you what you need to know by their verbal instructions to you. You need a good working knowledge of the English language, how to format documents, and an understanding of legal jargon. The formatting for wills and other legal documents is universal, so you just need to get your hands on some models to copy." Usually when you do a job for the first time, the lawyer or law office will give you a format to imitate. Soon formatting a legal document will be second nature to you!

Another very good way to gain experience as a legal word processor or transcriptionist is to take a course from a local business college. See the information on finding a business college near you in Chapter 3 for details.

Legal Secretary vs. Legal Transcriptionist

A legal secretary has contact with clients, keeps cases up to date, and keeps a calendar system for the law office. As you can see, a legal secretary pretty much has to work in a law office as opposed to working at home. On the other hand, legal transcriptionists use a Dictaphone and type up infor-

mation received on cassette tapes. You can do this work easily in the comfort of your own home!

It's also easy to do legal word processing at home. Nancy finds that she gets the bulk of her word processing work regarding personal injury cases. Her exact words were, "These cases are a real paper mill!" She also does word processing for criminal cases, contracts, and probate (wills).

You might find it beneficial to start out typing contracts, wills, and reports for lawyers, and then move on to transcription work once you have a better understanding of legal jargon. Transcription work can be extremely interesting when you understand what is being dictated—but if you don't, it can be very monotonous and boring!

Lawyers and Law Offices: What To Expect

General practitioners in law are gradually disappearing, just like general practitioners in medicine. Especially in large cities, you will tend to find firms that specialize in one particular area of the law, or large law firms that have many departments. Some common areas of specialization are corporation law, real estate law and foreclosures, probate matters, taxation, administrative law, and domestic relations.

As a legal transcriptionist, you too can specialize in a certain area of the law. We described above how Nancy specializes in typing reports about personal injury cases. How did she develop this as a specialty? Easy—she just started out doing it, her satisfied clients referred her to others, and the ball just kept rolling along!

As you can see, getting the first job is the trick. But it can be a lot easier than you think. Nancy started working in a law office just to do some typing in exchange for her rent. She didn't know she was going to become an expert on personal injury cases—it just happened! Call it luck or whatever you want, but the same kind of thing can happen to you. All you need to do is put yourself out there and believe in yourself, and you'll be amazed at the opportunities that come your way.

Mum's the Word

In Chapter 5 there is a complete explanation of confidentiality regarding medical transcription. The same rules apply for legal transcription. The information provided to you is highly confidential and must be treated as such at all times.

Literally everything you learn about a client or a case is confidential. You are bound by the same code of ethics as a lawyer. You must never talk about the cases you are typing with your friends or family, even if you leave out the names of the people involved.

Nancy's clients always hand deliver materials to her office to ensure confidentiality. Your clients may do the same, or they may ask you to pick up and deliver the work. Always be sure to work out an arrangement that guarantees confidentiality for everyone involved.

Transcription Dos and Don'ts

One thing that may surprise you at first is the sheer length of legal transcriptions. It's not unusual for lawyers to dictate for three to four hours on the same subject or case! That's one reason why it really helps if you understand what they are talking about. Otherwise, listening to a lawyer on tape will be like listening to someone speaking a foreign language—it can be a pretty baffling experience, and not much fun for you.

On the other hand, if you can follow the lawyer's train of thought, you'll find transcription a very pleasant task. Unlike doctors, most lawyers are very articulate and they express themselves extremely well. Usually it's much easier to follow a lawyer's dictation than a doctor's dictation. Sometimes lawyers tend to speak in very long sentences, and they can lose track of grammar and sentence structure. You can help them out by correcting any errors that you detect.

On some occasions it will be obvious to you that the lawyer has left out a word. If so, what you do is flag the omission and bring it to the lawyer's attention. Since there are probably many possibilities for what the missing word could be, never try to fill in the blank yourself. Instead, let the lawyer do it for you.

Pairs of Words that Sound Alike

Many words used in legal transcription sound alike when you hear them on tape. Some examples are:

Abjure, adjure
Adverse, averse
Avoid, void
Cost, costs
Persecute, prosecute
State, estate
Thereon, therein
Vendor, vendee

As you gain experience in dictation, you will become more familiar with the meaning of these words. You will definitely have an advantage if

you spend some time studying the meaning of these and other legal terms. You can find books to help you in your local library and bookstore. One useful reference is the *Legal Secretary's Complete Handbook*, which you can probably find at your local library. This book has a glossary of legal terms that will be of great benefit to you, especially if you are just starting out.

Repeated Material

One thing you'll notice about legal transcription work is that many phrases and paragraphs are used over and over again. The lawyer is usually so familiar with this material that he or she dictates it at a very high rate of speed. On the other hand, they may just say the first few words and let you, the transcriptionist, fill in the blanks while you are transcribing.

This is not something you should be worried about when you are first starting out as a transcriptionist. Soon you'll become familiar with the wording commonly used by the firm, and you'll be able to supply the needed material without a moment's hesitation.

Legal Instruments and Court Papers

A legal instrument is a term used to describe a formal written document, such as a deed, bill of sale, lease, contract, or will. The day-to-day operations of a law firm abound with the preparation of legal instruments. That means plenty of word processing and transcription work for you!

On the other hand, a court paper is prepared and filed solely for the information of the court. It is not a document that either party in a case is required to sign, but it is a vital part of the entire legal process. Court papers have a format all their own that involves special ruled paper and the use of "case captions." Law firms generate lots of court papers too, and you will be a step ahead of the game if you understand how to format them. Refer to a good legal secretary's handbook like the *Legal Secretary's Complete Handbook* for more information.

Legal instruments each have their own kinds of formats. Some examples are illustrated on the following pages. You will find a sample agreement form and the first and last pages of a sample will. These examples will give you an idea of what is required when typing a legal document.

Your Equipment

The equipment you need to specialize in legal word processing and transcription is really very basic: a dedicated word processor or computer, a word processing program like Microsoft Word or Word Perfect, and a transcribing machine. That's all the equipment Nancy needs, and she finds it works very well for her. In fact, she has both Microsoft Word and Word Perfect—some of her clients prefer one or the other, and she's able to keep them all happy!

Another home-based typist named Donna, who does word processing and transcription for both medical and legal clients, has this to say about equipment: "When you're first starting out, you can get used equipment advertised in the newspaper. Then buy and sell a few times to gradually move up in the quality of your equipment. Start out by doing some research in books and magazines. Don't buy thousands of dollars worth of equipment and then find yourself with no business!"

Donna also has both Microsoft Word and Word Perfect on her IBM-compatible. She feels it's good to have a variety of programs so you can switch from one to the other if you need to. She also says, "I keep everything on file for years for my clients. They will often ask for both a computer disk and a printout."

Donna is another home-based typist who learned by doing. She took basic business training all through high school and picked up a couple of refresher courses through adult education. When she first bought her computer she didn't know how to use it—she just taught herself! Now she charges $25 for her services, and she says, "What I do is so interesting, I love it. There is so much variety. I like the people I meet. And if I really don't want to do something, I have the choice."

Sample Will (First Page)

<u>THE LAST WILL AND TESTAMENT OF</u>

_____

I, _____ , of _____ , County of Belknap, State of New Hampshire, do hereby declare this my Last Will and Testament, and hereby revoke any and all wills and codicils heretofore made by me.

FIRST: I direct that all of my just debts and funeral expenses be paid as soon as practicable after my decease.

SECOND: I give and devise my farm located in the town of Meredith, County of Belknap, State of New Hampshire, to my son, <u>Richard</u>, and his heirs and assigns forever.

THIRD: I give and bequeath to my daughter, <u>Anne</u>, fifty (50) shares of common stock of United States Steel, Inc.

FOURTH: I give and bequeath the following sums of money to the following persons, to-wit:

(a) The sum of Seven Hundred Fifty Dollars ($750.) to <u>Robert Jones</u> of Allentown, Georgia.

(b) The sum of One Thousand Dollars ($1,000.) to <u>Edna Jones</u> of Ellisville, Florida.

FIFTH: I give and bequeath to the <u>Merchants' Loan and Trust</u> <u>Company</u>, a coporation, organized under the laws of

-1-

Sample Will (Last Page)

made in this will and including any property over which I have a power of

appointment, hereby defined as my residuary estate, I give, devise and

bequeath to my daughter, <u>Jane</u>, her heirs and assigns forever.

     IN WITNESS WHEREOF, I have signed my name at the end of this

my Last Will and Testament and affixed my seal this   day of May, 19—.

_____ [L.S.]

    The foregoing instrument, consisting of ten typewritten
pages, including this page, was signed, published and
declared by _____ to be his Last Will and
Testament in the presence of us, who, at his request, in his
presence and in the presence of each other, have subscribed
our names as witnesses.

_____ of _____

_____ of _____

_____ of _____

Sample Agreement

THIS AGREEMENT, entered into on the ___ day of
_____, 19—, by and between _____ CORPORATION,
a corporation organized and existing under and by virtue of
the laws of the State of _____, and having its office
at _____, _____, hereinafter referred to as
"_____," and THE _____ COMPANY, a corporation organized and existing under and by virtue of the laws of the
State of _____, and having its office at _____,
_____, hereinafter referred to as "_____,"

W I T N E S S E T H :

WHEREAS _____

_____; and

WHEREAS _____

_____

_____.

NOW, THEREFORE, in consideration of the premises

_____

_____,

IT IS AGREED:

1. _____

_____

_____ .

2. _____

_____.

IN WITNESS WHEREOF the parties hereto have on the
day and year first above written caused these presents to be
executed in their behalf and in their corporate names re-
spectively by their proper officers hereunto duly authorized
and their respective corporate seals to be hereto attached
by like authority.

(Corporate Seal)   _____CORPORATION

                                    ,By _____
ATTEST: President

_____
           Secretary   THE _____COMPANY

(Corporate Seal)   By _____
                                         Vice President
ATTEST:

_____
           Secretary

Getting Your First Client

No matter where you live, there are lawyers out there with plenty of work for you. As we said earlier in this chapter, the easiest way to break in is to start by working in a law office in some capacity, even if only for a short time. A year or two should be more than sufficient to get you familiar with the field.

Then, when you leave your job to start out on your own, let all the lawyers in the firm know what you are doing. Give each one of them your new business card. Since you know how they like to do things and you've probably done typing for at least a few of them directly, you'll be first in line when there's a rush job and no one in the office has time to do it.

There's a sample letter on the next page. You can use this kind of letter to approach lawyers who you don't know. Use your local yellow pages and be very systematic—contact each attorney listed. Send them a letter, wait a week, and then make a follow-up phone call to find out if they need your expert typing assistance.

Here are some other ideas to use when searching for new clients:

• Write a short press release which states who you are, what you have to offer, and how you can be contacted. Send this press release to all the local newspapers. (See sample press release on page 80.)

• Your local newspaper will carry notices of new lawyers who are just opening their offices. Call or send a letter to let them know about your new typing and transcription service. (See sample letter on page 79.)

You Have Nothing to Lose!

Legal word processing and transcription is a great career that's just waiting to happen. The lawyers and law firms are all around you. Once they become familiar with the service you offer, you'll have all the business you can handle!

Just remember, always do the very best job you can at all times. Take the time to educate yourself, whether it's by taking an entry-level job at a law firm or by enrolling in the appropriate classes at your local business college or adult education program. Soon, like Nancy and Donna, you too will be charging $25 an hour and looking forward to the short commute from your bedroom to your home office when you get up in the morning. Like Donna says, "It's actually good to work out of the home. More and more people are doing it. It cuts costs and insurance, too. It's really a nice way to go!"

Sample Letter

Today's Date

John H. Banks, Esq.
Banks and Banks, Attorneys at Law
400 North Street
Big City, USA 11111

Dear Mr. Banks:

After working as an office assistant for the legal offices of Leed and Cole, I have recently opened my own legal word processing and transcription business.

I can provide you with fast, accurate service for all your legal typing needs. My business card is enclosed. My regular office hours are from 8 am to 5 pm, but my answering machine is on at all hours. I also pick up and deliver and offer one-day turnaround on rush jobs.

I will give you a call next week to inquire if you have a need for my services at this time. Thank you for your consideration, and I look forward to speaking with you soon.

Sincerely,

(signature)

Tina Smith
Tina's Typing Service
200 Garden St.
Any Town, USA 19101
xxx-xxx-xxxx

Sample Press Release

Today's Date

FOR IMMEDIATE RELEASE

Contact:
Tina Smith
Tina's Typing Service
200 Garden St.
Any Town, USA 19101
xxx-xxx-xxxx

SMITH OPENS TYPING SERVICE

Any Town, USA—Tina Smith announces that she has opened Tina's Typing Service, specializing in legal word processing and transcription.

Smith has worked for the Any Town law firm of Leed and Cole for the past two years. She trained in the legal transcription program at Any Town Business College.

The new business offers free pick-up and delivery service to all law firms in Any Town. For more information, call Tina's Typing Service at xxx-xxxx.

###

For more information, contact Tina's Typing Service, 200 Garden St., Any Town, USA 19101; xxx-xxx-xxxx.

Chapter 7:
Desktop Publishing

Publishing used to be an industry unto itself. If you wanted to print up a book, you had to go through a great many steps. First, you had to take your manuscript to a special typist called a typesetter. Then the typed version would go to a paste-up person, who would get the manuscript ready for the printer. Any corrections you needed had to be retyped and pasted in by hand. Then, finally, the book would go to the printer. The whole process seemed to take an eternity!

Nowadays, these time-consuming steps have been completely eliminated by a phenomenon called desktop publishing. Desktop publishing allows you to combine text and graphics into a single document. Just about anyone with a personal computer can use desktop publishing software to produce professional quality books, newsletters, flyers, and other printed materials. As a home-based typist, you may definitely want to consider adding this service to your business!

This chapter will discuss the equipment you need and the options you have for finding work in this exciting field. The profit potential is very large. You can easily charge $25-$35 an hour, and sometimes $45 or more in major metropolitan areas. Plus, the more computer programs you know, the more you can charge. So read on and learn what your future in desktop publishing can hold!

Mac or IBM?

The Macintosh computer is generally considered the king of desktop publishing. But that doesn't mean you can't do desktop publishing on IBM—you can. It's just that most professionals who specialize in desktop publishing prefer Macs. Why?

First of all, the Macintosh computer was more or less designed for

desktop publishing. It is very easy to use. Many programs are available for the Mac that are very beneficial to desktop publishers. For many years Pagemaker, one of the most popular desktop publishing programs, was only available on the Mac.

Graphic designers are especially loyal to the Mac. Programs like Adobe Photoshop enable you to do special effects with photographs, and Aldus Freehand allows you to draw your own illustrations and logos. If you are artistic, you will definitely want to check out these programs! Knowing these programs will take you to the top of the pay scale for desktop publishing.

On the other hand, if all you are interested in doing is producing basic newsletters for your clients, you can do that just fine on an IBM or IBM clone. These days, because of Windows, the user interface for IBM is much easier than it's ever been. Pagemaker for Windows now allows IBM-based users to enjoy the same desktop publishing features that Mac users have had all along.

So if you need an IBM system to take care of the word processing part of your business, rest assured that all you need is Pagemaker to add desktop publishing to your services. But if you plan to make desktop publishing the mainstay of your business, definitely consider investing in a Macintosh system. The startup costs may be higher, but down the road you'll thank yourself for it many times over!

Desktop Publishing Services

Here are just a few of the many services you can offer your clients as a desktop publisher. To produce any one of these items, you have a great number of typefaces to choose from to give each piece a custom look.

- Flyers. You can design flyers for any occasion or special event. You can make them one or two sided and add "clip art" that you get ready to use on a computer disk or CD-ROM.

- Brochures. You can make them any size you want, though the most common size is an 8 1/2 x 11 inch sheet of paper folded in thirds. You can add photographs or artwork, a company logo, and any other bells and whistles you want to make your brochures stand out in a crowd!

- Newsletters. More than 100,000 newsletters are published in the United States every year. With desktop publishing, you can produce a great-looking newsletter even if your client has a shoestring budget. (Hint: Collect as many sample newsletters as you can to get ideas before you begin.)

- Reports and Manuals. Business reports and company manuals often include graphs, charts, and artwork of many kinds. Desktop publishing makes them look their professional best.

- Booklets and Books. Whether they be small or large, booklets and books are a snap to produce via desktop publishing. Pagemaker has automatic page numbering, indexing, table of contents, and many other special features that simplify the process.

Your Local Copy Shop

Once you have created your document, you can either have copies made from the master at your local copy shop, or—if your client has a big enough budget—take the job to a bona fide printer. I definitely recommend using your local copy shop as your printer of choice for all but the most sophisticated jobs.

Get to know the folks at your local copy shop. Pay them a visit and ask them to tell you about all the services they offer. You'll probably be surprised at how many different kinds of paper there are to choose from, and at how little it costs to copy, collate, fold, and staple your job. National chains tend to offer the most services, and Kinkos is one of the best. But do some research by visiting several copy shops in your area to find the one you like. Then bring them all your business and establish a long-term relationship with them.

Where to Get Training

Just about every community college and adult education program offers classes in desktop publishing. They are so popular that often the classes have waiting lists. In my town they have a lottery every time because so many people want to take the class.

If you really want to go full steam ahead, take a look at certificate programs in desktop publishing. They are often offered through local universities or business colleges. You complete a series of courses on desktop publishing and receive a certificate at the end of the series. This is the perfect way to get advanced training in desktop publishing services, including graphics programs like Aldus Freehand and Adobe Photoshop—though it may be overkill if all you want to do is flyers and newsletters. You might find, as I did, that the best way to enter this field is to learn by doing!

How I Became A Desktop Publisher

Personally, I never took a class in desktop publishing—in fact, I've never even read a manual about it!—and it has been an important part of my business for many years. I bought my first Macintosh computer, a Mac Plus, in 1987. Some of the people I worked with had them and knew how to use them, and I would just hang around and watch them work. I asked lots of questions and then tried out the computer on my own.

Even though the Mac Plus was very primitive back then, I could see it was the wave of the future. Within a year after I bought my own computer, I quit my job and went out on my own. I didn't have a laser printer— I just had a dot matrix printer at home—so to get final copies of all the brochures and flyers and books I was producing, I would go down to a local "service bureau" and rent computer time there to use the laser printers. Today you too can do the same thing at many copy shops, like Kinkos mentioned earlier. (Though chances are if you have a word processor or computer, you already have a laser printer of your own!)

Whenever a new version of Pagemaker or some other important program came out, I would find someone who knew how to use it and pick up pointers from them. The people at the service bureau were always very helpful as well. That was all the education I ever needed in desktop publishing—and if I can do it that way, you can, too!

Scanners

Scanners take text, graphics, and photographs and translate them onto computer disks so you can import them into your desktop publishing program. As a desktop publisher, there are two kinds of scanners you need to know about. One, called an OCR scanner (for Optical Character Recognition), allows you to take text that was typed somewhere else and make it into a computer file. This can be useful if there are many pages of text you need to work with (for example, page after page of addresses) that you have a printout for but no computer disk. It will save you from retyping the whole list. OCR scanners keep getting better, but keep in mind that to be really effective, the document to be scanned must be in very good condition.

The other most common scanner is a flatbed scanner, which is used to turn artwork and photographs into computer files. You can then bring the images into your desktop publishing program and place them wherever you want in your document. (And after you place them, you can make them

bigger or smaller, redraw them, crop them or do whatever is necessary to get the look you want!)

Scanners are fairly expensive pieces of equipment. If you're just starting out as a desktop publisher, you'll want to use the scanners at your local copy shop or computer service bureau. The charge is usually very minimal, though it may cost you more to scan especially large or complicated images.

Laser Printers

A laser printer is really helpful for your own desktop publishing business. You can get by without one by taking your computer disk to a service bureau or copy shop that rents time on computers. But it's so much better just to push a button and have the finished pages come pouring out of your very own laser printer.

The ideal would be to have a laser printer with a resolution, or print quality, of 300 dots per inch. This book uses a laser printer with even higher quality, 600 dots per inch. As you might expect, the print quality is twice as good, but it costs almost twice as much—and besides, for most purposes, 300 dots per inch is the standard.

Ink jet printers fall a little lower on the quality scale than a real laser printer, while dot matrix printers are not acceptable. Since you will need at least an ink jet printer for your word processing business, try to spend a little more for a real laser printer if you intend to do any desktop publishing. The resulting quality will set you apart and help you grow your business that much faster.

What About Quark Express?

Quark Express is another desktop publishing program for the Macintosh that is worth mentioning here. Quark is a very powerful program with sophisticated features, and many desktop publishing professionals prefer it. However, it is much harder to learn than Pagemaker.

So unless you decide to enroll in a certificate program for desktop publishing (where they will probably require that you take a class in Quark), I recommend that you stick with Pagemaker. Whereas you can figure out how to use Pagemaker almost as soon as you install it on your computer, the same is not true of Quark. (Believe me, I've tried it!) My motto is, why suffer? Take the path of least resistance—and in this case, that means Pagemaker!

It is true that some of your potential clients may work in Quark and prefer that you do too—for example, advertising agencies or graphic designers. But for the most part, it is only the very specialized client that will ask you to work in Quark. If you're not sure, ask around before you invest any money in computer software. A little research in advance will help you make the right decision.

Discover Paper Direct

One of the best resources around to help put your desktop publishing business on the map is Paper Direct. This company offers a full line of full color, preprinted papers that you can use to produce brochures, business cards, certificates, letterhead, envelopes, newsletters, presentation folders, and more for your clients.

When you use these papers, you run them through your laser printer to and come out with the finished product on the spot. Every catalog has wonderful new products to choose from. There is a design to suit every mood and every client! To order your free catalog, call 1-800-A-PAPERS.

Finding Work

It's easy to find work as a desktop publisher—so easy, in fact, that you'll find yourself turning work away before too long! Here are some ideas to get you going.

First of all, think of all the people you know who belong to organizations, from the PTA to garden clubs to sports and civic organizations. Make a list of names with the organization written in beside them. Then call up your friends and tell them that you're ready to produce fliers and brochures for the organizations they belong to. Give them a special introductory offer if you like—say, half price for the first job. I guarantee you'll get lots of takers!

The next thing you can do is get a business card and put it up at your local copy shop and computer service bureau. Think of other places to post your card around town. You may find bulletin boards in coffee shops and even in office buildings. And don't forget your local laundromat!

If you already have a home typing business, send a postcard or letter to all your existing clients to let them know about the exciting new desktop publishing services you offer. Soon word of mouth will take over, and that's the best advertising of all! Use the sample letter on the next page to get you started.

Sample Promotional Letter

Today's Date

Bill Businessman
XYZ Corporation
2001 Main St.
Any Town, USA 44005

Dear Mr. Businessman:
Tammy Hughes Word Processing Service now offers a full line of desktop publishing services! Tammy is fully equipped to bring you the best service and prices on the following items:

- Flyers
- Brochures
- Newsletters
- Reports and Manuals
- Booklets and Books

Tammy will personally help you ensure that all your documents look their professional best. Call for more information and your FREE quote today at xxx-xxxx. And as a special introductory offer, you'll receive 20% off on every order placed by March 31!

So don't delay—give Tammy Hughes Word Processing Service a call today, and have professional-looking documents in your office tomorrow!

Sincerely,

(signature)

Tammy Hughes, Owner
Tammy Hughes Word Processing Service

You might also want to consider running a small classified ad in the services directory of your local newspaper. Try it for a week or two and see if you get results. Keep it simple—even "Desktop Publishing" and your phone number would be sufficient for starters.

So now, decide which of these ideas you like the best. Take your top three favorites and implement them as work-finding strategies right away. Both you and your pocketbook will be glad you did!

Define Your Niche

Another strategy you can use to find work is to pick a niche and devote your self-promotion efforts to seeking work in that niche. For example, your niche might be newsletters. Put the words "Newsletter Specialist" on all of your advertising. You might even put it on your business card.

This is a great way to let people know that when they come to you, they come to a real expert in the field. They will bypass other advertisers and call you first.

Here's to Your Success!

Desktop publishing has been the key to many successful home-based businesses. I personally know a dozen people or more who work out of their homes doing desktop publishing. These people wouldn't have it any other way.

Lana D. used to have her own office doing desktop publishing downtown. Then she closed up her business for awhile and worked for a big company instead. Now she works at home, and that big company is one of her biggest clients—plus she has many other clients as well! She turned the whole situation around, and now she has the best of both worlds.

Lana says, "Working at home is the best thing I've ever done. On busy days I use a courier service to deliver jobs across town. They charge just $3-$5 per delivery and it saves me lots of time. Things have gone so well that I just recently bought all new computer equipment to serve my clients even better."

If the idea of creating documents that combine text and graphics appeals to you, then desktop publishing will satisfy you like no other kind of typing will. Take the plunge and explore this exciting addition to your business—you won't regret it!

Chapter 8:
Getting Ready
For Success

Now it's time to start prioritizing the steps you will take to get your home-based typing service up and running. Don't let this overwhelm you. Read this chapter and firmly tell yourself that each task, when broken down individually, is really quite simple. Don't look too far ahead or you might find yourself saying *"This is too difficult! I don't have all the skills to run a business! I'd better just keep doing what I've been doing, it's easier. It's safer ....."*

Nonsense! Remember, every successful business began the very same way. Someone had an idea, devised a plan, completed each task that had to be done, and opened their door for business. *You can do the same thing!*

A perfect example is Nancy Browning, now one of the most sought after experts on stained glass designs. Nancy had always been interested in art, but as a single mother with two young daughters to support she had put every ounce of energy into her job as the manager of a retail crafts store. At the suggestion of a friend, she enrolled in a stained glass class at her local Adult Education program.

Nancy loved making stained glass windows and jewelry and soon began selling her work to earn extra money. Frustrated with the limited number and type of patterns available in her store, she began to design her own. Soon, other students in her class were asking for her original designs. While at the copy shop one afternoon making yet another pattern copy, her then nine year old daughter Melody said "Mom, why don't you sell those?"

The rest, as they say, is history. Nancy began her own home-based business by copying her designs and selling them to other craft stores and to students in the Adult Ed classes. Today, Nancy no longer works in a retail store, but has a fully equipped office in her converted basement where she designs, markets, packages, and ships her patterns all over the world!

But just in case you're having some (perfectly normal) nervous jitters about starting your own home-based business, let's take a moment and surprise yourself by finding out how well suited you really are to being your own boss. By answering Yes or No to each of the following questions your feelings about owning your own typing service will begin to emerge:

_____	**I always try to look at things from both sides**
_____	**People notice how conscientious I am**
_____	**I like taking some professional risks**
_____	**I am usually quite creative**
_____	**I am self-motivated**
_____	**Rejection hurts but doesn't stop me**
_____	**I try to be honest in all my relationships**
_____	**People seem to think I'm quite smart**
_____	**I am a hard worker**
_____	**I have definite life goals in mind**
_____	**I like a challenge**

If you answered yes to half or more of these questions, you are definitely a candidate for self-employment. If you had more no's than yeses, this simply means that perhaps you need to take a little more time to learn all about owning a typing service.

It's quite possible that you simply don't yet have enough job related experience and need a few additional skills before you begin. Don't be the least bit intimidated by this, it's a good sign that you are a very careful, well-rounded thinker, able to look at all sides of a situation. This type of conservative fact gathering will be very valuable when you *are* the boss, responsible for making good decisions relating to your business.

Now let's get ready to begin our first assignment—to create a business plan for you. Sound like a lot of work? It's really quite simple. Your business plan is a working guide to your typing service. Your plan will be constantly changing as your business changes and grows.

Right now, let's make a list of the things you need to purchase, and add to that list a spiral bound notebook. This will be your working manual. Keep it close by at all times so that whenever you think of an idea, or something that needs to be done, you can write it down. This notebook can also hold your first business plan. So now, let's do this together.

Your Business Plan

Your business plan will help you to answer these questions:

- **What Are My Personal Goals?**
- **Who Will My Customers Be?**
- **How Much Money Do I Need?**
- **How Will I Advertise?**
- **Who Is My Competition?**
- **What Are My Start-up Costs?**
- **How Will I Charge My Clients?**
- **How Will I Keep My Records?**

One of the most worrisome questions for new business owners is: *"How much will it cost to start my business?"* Let's look back at Nancy and her stained glass designs again.

She proudly tells people today that she spent less that one hundred dollars to get her business off the ground, and the majority of that was in opening her business checking account, getting a city license, and having business cards and envelopes printed. She kept her cash expenditures to the minimum by only reproducing the patterns as she received orders.

The smart business owner never spends money until she absolutely has to! Get in the habit of looking for alternative ways of getting things done, and don't be afraid to ask family, friends and neighbors for ideas and help.

How Much Will It Cost?

Reducing this worry is quite simple if you start putting your ideas and the facts down on paper. Once the information is in black and white right in front of you, it no longer seems such a mystery. Understand that the following list doesn't mean that you will immediately have to invest in each and every item, it's simply a good way for you to begin calculating the amount of money you'll need to get started.

ITEM	ESTIMATED COST
Business license	_____
Business cards, letterhead,	_____
Envelopes	_____
Business telephone	_____
Consulting fees (tax, legal, etc.)	_____
Office equipment (computer, FAX, copier)	_____
Office furnishings (desk, filing cabinets, etc.)	_____
Answering machine or Voice Mail	_____
Initial Advertising, Marketing & Promotion	_____

There are many options available besides just laying out cash (which you may not have readily available) in order to get the doors open for business. Some entrepreneurs have successfully implemented one or all of the following plans. You may even have a more creative plan of you own!

Plan A

Keep your present job and begin moonlighting your new business. If you commit to spending at least 16 hours a week on your new business, although it may take a little longer to begin earning the kind of money you need to, you will also minimize the financial risks and take the pressure off. You can also funnel some of your regular income into the new business to finance purchases of equipment. *(Note: it is quite difficult for a new business to borrow money from a bank or other conventional lending institution. Keeping your job can therefore help secure a loan to get your business off the ground.)*

Since I've always been the one to keep the family finances in order, I was very cautious about leaving my job to become a full-time freelance writer. My husband was the one always encouraging me to take the chance and do what I really loved, and wanted to do. But I had financial goals in mind, and I wanted to be sure I could continue to contribute to my family's financial needs.

Now that I can look back over my years as an independent business owner, I can honestly say that I wish I'd done it sooner, been a little braver and taken the chance. On a scale of one to ten, my self-employment years have been a nine! Yours can be too.

Trust your instincts and have faith in your mind, which does most of life's hard work on its own time! As you think deeply and do your research for your new venture, let your mind wander freely and work on the whole idea while you're doing other things. Your mind will soon provide you with all the answers you need to make a good decision.

Plan B

If your husband or wife is employed, sit down together and determine how you can best cut your overall living expenses so that you can live on one income until your business is showing a profit.

Remember that you won't have commuting, lunch, clothing or possibly child care expenses when working from your home. Perhaps you could even make greater use of your washing machine instead of sending things to the dry cleaners, or take up some of the gardening and yard work instead of paying someone else to do it.

Here's a great exercise. Get out your check register and list every check you've written, and how much it was for in the last three months. Look at those *extra* expenses closely and I'll bet you'll find at least one area that you had no idea you were spending that much money on! When I did this, I was amazed to find the number of checks made out for pizza delivery. I immediately decreased the number of times we had pizza each month. I'm sure you'll find certain areas you can economize on too.

Plan C

Reduce your hours at your present job from full to part-time to provide at least *some* steady income while you build up your new business. If at all possible, start looking at your current employer and professional contacts for future clients.

The ideal situation would be to turn your current employer into your first paying client. That's exactly what Peter Bolton did when he decided to leave his job as a bank teller. Peter was a budding playwright, but his nine to five work schedule left little time or creative energy for writing. He knew how crazy things were at the end of every month at the bank, and arranged to work only the week before the books were closed, on Saturdays, and on-call when other employees called in sick or were on vacation. He managed to budget his living expenses so that his bank job still met his needs and gave him time to pursue his writing career.

Let's say you've calculated the amount of money you'll need to start your new venture. It's not that much, but *you just don't happen to have the money!* Don't despair. The two most important traits for an entrepreneur to have are *flexibility* and *creativity*. It's better to learn right now that money and how you earn it and spend it is always going to be one of the most important issues in owning your own business. Sometimes you'll have a lot ..... sometimes you'll wonder how to keep the lights turned on. Money manipulation is one of the primary rules of self-employment.

Where Do I Get The Money?

So if you find yourself short of the funds needed to get your typing service off the ground, what can you do? Where do you go to get it? If you just answered, *"I'll just wait until I have enough money saved!"* you may need to rethink your commitment to being in business for yourself.

If, on the other hand your mind immediately began searching for possible sources of cash, you've just cleared one of the biggest hurdles to becoming a self-employed business owner. Let me help you by sharing a few of the ideas given to me by other entrepreneurs who were once in the very same position. Try raising that extra money by:

- **Life Insurance Policy Equity**
- **Home Equity Loan**
- **Credit Union**
- **Friends**
- **Family**
- **Savings**
- **Retirement Funds**
- **Inheritance**
- **Hold A Garage Sale**
- **Employment Bonus**
- **Credit Card**
- **Kids College Fund**
- **Stocks**
- **You Could Even Sell Something!**

In other words, we mustn't let a lack of money keep us from our dreams. Money comes and money goes, so decide right now to make it work for you. If you have trouble taking money from the equity in your life insurance policy, just think of it as a more immediate *investment* strategy.

Don't jeopardize yourself or your family's financial security, but in the same vein, don't use a lack of cash as an excuse to not do something that you really want to do and that in the long run, may be the most financially rewarding opportunity you've ever seized! Remember that you are by far your most important asset. Invest in yourself and it will probably prove to be the *best* investment you'll ever make!

More Financing Tips

A few more thoughts on financing your new business. If you must borrow money, borrow the *minimum* amount you need and then only to finance equipment or other supplies that will pay for themselves through the work that you do. In the early days of setting up your business, you don't want the pressure of a monthly loan payment hanging over your head.

Become familiar with the term *"Bootstrapping,"* the process of buying only that which you *absolutely must have*, when you must have it, to keep you in business. The beauty of bootstrapping is that you will *never* buy expensive equipment, invest in untested advertising programs, or put yourself out on a risky financial limb.

The downside of this strategy is that your business will probably not grow as quickly because your growth will be restricted by the actual amount of business that you can generate. The upside is that the more carefully you grow your business, the sounder it will be. Plus you have the added advantage of learning everything as you go.

Ideally you will get your business off the ground with the money you have on hand, i.e. money that is not earmarked for any specific need. This could include business or contracts that you can generate immediately, existing cash on hand (savings) or credit card borrowing.

If you plan to keep your job for awhile, it may be possible to change your federal income tax withholding and use the additional cash to put into your business. Check with your tax specialist or accountant to find out how best to utilize and keep records of this particular strategy. *This was exactly how the owner of this publishing company began his own business twenty years ago, it too was a totally shoestring, bootstrapped venture!*

Be sure to also think about your possible future financial needs. If borrowing is in the picture, make the arrangements before you leave your job. Let's say you want to increase your credit limit on a Master Card or Visa to use for business purposes. Make sure to apply to the bank before that farewell party at your office. Credit lending policies can be more strict for the self-employed.

How Much Money Do I Need To Make?

This is a very important question, and the answer is crucial to getting ready for success. It's time to sit down with pen and paper and list your current monthly income and how it's now being spent. Make sure that you list *all* of the associated costs of going to work if you are now employed, as these expenses will be deducted from your net monthly income when you become self-employed. Your monthly expenses may include:

Monthly Expense	$ Cost
Rent/Mortgage Payment	_____
Auto loans, maintenance & gas	_____
Food	_____
Clothes	_____
Medical & Dental care	_____
Utilities	_____
Insurance (health/life/car)	_____
Entertainment & Gifts	_____
Other - Miscellaneous	_____
Total Living Expenses	_____

How Much Should I Charge?

Experience has shown that it is much better to underestimate the actual number of hours you may be able to work, rather than assuming that as in your old job you will be putting in a regular 40-hour week.

It's important to remember that not all of your time will be spent typing, as there are numerous other things that you will need to take care of to keep your business running smoothly—things like networking with other professionals, bookkeeping, advertising and marketing activities. Many self-employed typists find that there are times where they have no work at all. In fact, this is actually a good thing, since it gives you the opportunity to work on soliciting new clients and attend meetings and networking groups (more about Networking in Chapter 12) that will help build your client roster.

Even in today's Fax-mad world, where everything seems to be sent over the phone wires, nothing can take the place of a face-to-face meeting with a potential customer that you're trying to get to sign on with you. Having tried all sorts of methods to attract new business, I can attest to the fact that in many cases it is my personality and enthusiasm that finally convince new clients that they really do need me!

Now it's time to seek out local and national trade organizations (they're listed in the References at the back of this book) to find out what the going rate is for contracted typing. It's also a good idea to pull out those Yellow Pages again and call your competition to find out what they're charging. You don't need to identify yourself as the new kid on the block, simply ask what their hourly rate is and if possible, could they send you a price list or brochure about their services. This will give you a leg-up in setting a realistic price for your services.

Once you've determined the average price for typing services in your area—let's say it's $15.00 per hour—you can then multiply the hourly rate by the number of hours you work to determine your monthly income. This gets a little more complicated when you understand that you must also incorporate non-billable time (the hours you are doing marketing, bookkeeping, etc.) in addition to your cost of doing business.

Let's say you need to net (after business expenses) $1,000 per month. Here's an easy formula for helping you determine how much to charge per hour, and how many hours you will need to work each month to meet your income goals.

$15.00/hour X 25 (billable) hours	= $375 per week
(X) 4 weeks	= $1500/month (gross income)
(–) operating expenses of $500 per month	= $1000 net income

This calculation is based on working a 40-hour week, 25 of those hours spent actually typing, 15 hours spent taking care of the other administrative tasks I mentioned earlier. Also note that your operating expenses should include taxes, insurance, supplies, loan payments, postage, equipment leasing, repairs, and maintenance.

Chapter 9: Things To Do

Now that we've talked about what it's going to take for you to set up your home-based typing/word processing business, it's time for us to take action. I've designed this section to be your step-by-step guide to getting the doors open for business. In this section we'll cover the absolute necessities for getting your business off on the right track. It's now time to purchase your day-planner, the kind with multiple sections, pockets and files so that you can keep the launch of your new business organized and on schedule.

Name Your Baby

Choosing a name for your business may be one of the most important (and most fun!) things you will do. Most people choose to set up business independently, without partners. This is known as a *Sole Proprietorship*.

If you do plan on having a partner in your business, or decide to incorporate immediately, for your own protection I suggest that you seek the advice of an attorney. If you have chosen to own and operate the business strictly by yourself, you may wish to simply use your own name as the business name. For example:

Mary Jones Typing Service

Using your own name for the business offers many advantages, including simplicity and ease of remembering. It also eliminates the need for getting a Fictitious Business Name Statement (also known as FBN or DBA - Doing Business As). If you choose a name other than your own for your business,—such as *Wonder Words, SOS Word Processing, or Tammy's Typing*, that name must be registered with the appropriate governmental offices. Using your own name for the business simplifies the whole process, and also reduces your expenses by not having to file and pay for a Fictitious

Business Name Statement.

I met a woman last year while waiting in the doctor's office, and we started talking about what we did, how busy we were, and how we really wanted to get out of there. She told me she was an accountant with a local firm, and was thinking about becoming independent and working at home.

Of course, I was all ears! She asked if she could pick my brain sometime, since this was all pretty new to her. We met for lunch a few weeks later, and her biggest question was whether she should use her own name for the business, or try and make one up. Since we live in a pretty small town, my immediate question was: did people know her name, and associate it with what she did? *"Oh, yes! In fact I'll keep most of my clients since my boss is looking to downsize and reduce his workload."*

Well, that answered that question. When I told her about having to get an FBN, and the immediate value her name recognition would bring to her new home-based business, she was convinced. Here's the really good part: she is now my accountant, and I'm thrilled to be able to give my business to another home-based worker.

If you do decide to use a name other than your own, you'll need to contact your local County Clerk's office at City Hall. The laws in each state, county, township, etc. can be very different. A great source of information for small, independent businesses is your local Chamber of Commerce, Small Business Administration (SBA), and Service Corps of Retired Executives (SCORE); please see the Resources section at the end of the book for addresses and phone numbers.

I've been very lucky to have met a wonderful mentor through SCORE. Jack not only knows *almost* everything about running a business, he's also become a member of my family and joins us for all holidays and family get-togethers. Through Jack, I've also met other retired executives who have a wealth of knowledge and experience and are just a phone call away.

Likewise the Small Business Administration (SBA) was established by the United States government in 1953 as an independent agency to aid, counsel, and protect all interests of small businesses. In 1981 Congress defeated an attempt to abolish the SBA, and although funding has declined slightly, there are still many programs available to assist you. The SBA provides loans for business expansion and improvement, and also attempts to increase the number of government contracts granted to individuals who operate small businesses. The Minority Small Business program is dedicated to increasing the number of minority and women owned businesses, and also sponsors programs to help small business owners develop management skills. If you are interested in SBA loan programs, your first step will be to contact your local bank and find out the steps needed to apply.

Please also note that if you use a Fictitious Business Name (FBN), a legal notice must be published in the newspaper. When you file for your FBN, those instructions usually come with the paperwork. Remember too that when using a name other than your own, you will be required to give the bank a copy of the FBN filing in order to open a business checking account. Using your own name as that of your business will eliminate this step, and your business checking account can be opened in your own name, using just your Social Security Number for tax reporting purposes.

If for any reason you don't have a Social Security Number, simply phone your nearest IRS or Social Security office and ask for form #SS-5. Once it's filled out and you've shown your Birth Certificate or other acceptable proof of birth, the card will be issued.

Getting Your Business License

Every person running a business *must* have a Business License. This is usually very easy, and nowhere near as expensive as it sounds! You can apply for your Business License immediately, but again, if your business has a name other than your own, you will need to present your FBN at the time you apply for a license.

Most Business Licenses are issued by your city, county, parish or township. Simply go there (look in the White Pages of your phone book under Government to find the location), fill out the forms, pay the annual fee and you're officially licensed by the city. *(Note: the annual licensing fee is usually based on your expected business sales for the upcoming year. Be very conservative and estimate on the low side. Once your business is up and running, you can always adjust as necessary.)*

Things can get a little more complicated if where you live has certain restrictions on running a business out of your home. That's because most residential areas don't want to be impacted with trucks and traffic noise. A home based typing business doesn't usually pose any of these problems, but you may be asked to pay an additional fee for a zoning variance or conditional use permit.

Again, your local city officials will have all of this information. A simple phone call (perhaps anonymous) is all it takes to find out where you stand and what you will need to do.

Opening Your Business Checking Account

There are many reasons to open a separate checking account for your new business, not the least of which is the fact that it makes you a *real* business. Even though the IRS does not require you to have a separate account for income tax purposes, should your business ever be audited, this type of account will help you prove your business intent.

For record keeping and future planning, being able to look back over actual income deposits and to whom you paid what for supplies, will be a tangible record of how your business is doing. With the tax deductions available to home-based businesses, it is very important that you are able to prove that you paid for certain items (supplies, utilities, insurance, etc.) from your business and not your personal account. A cancelled check from your business account is the easiest way to do this. So please, do not overlook this important and tangibly satisfying step in getting your business open.

Assuming that you do decide to operate your typing business as a sole proprietorship, you will be the only person to sign checks on your business checking account. However, I strongly recommend that you choose one other person that you trust to also have the right to sign checks should the need arise. You just never know when you might be traveling on business, or ill and unable to carry on business as usual.

Generally, a spouse or family member would be your first choice, but if you have an accountant or other professional person willing to accept the responsibility, that could work just fine. I have both my husband and my

grown daughter on my account, since any of us could be out of town when a check needs to be written. I've given each of them a supply of checks, so that if I need them to pick up something for me, they don't even have to come over to get one.

For the newly created business, thrift and economy are buzzwords we need to keep in mind. You will probably not be generating much activity on your checking account at first, so there is no need to choose an elaborate type of checkbook. The single checkbook, just like the one you probably use for your personal account, will be more than adequate. It will also be easy to carry in your purse or pocket, rather than trying to drag one of those big notebook styles around.

Choose the simplest (and least expensive) check design and always include your business address (not a P.O. Box!) and phone number on the checks. Be sure to start your checks with at least number 1001, never 101 as that is an immediate indication that your business is brand new and probably very small! Even though that may be true, you still want to be seen as credible by the people you will be writing checks to.

It might also be helpful if you plan to do your own bookkeeping to get the type of checks that have carbon copies of each check included in the book. This way if you ever forget what you wrote the check for or who it was to, the information will be right there in your checkbook.

Once you begin transacting business it's a good idea to get in the habit of paying yourself a salary (no matter how small it may be at first!) on a weekly or bimonthly basis. The best way to do this is to write yourself a check, made payable to CASH and deposit it into your personal account. This will stop you from writing checks for personal bills and grocery store runs on your business account. For your own accounting and tax purposes, use your business checking account *only* for business! *Reminder:* Never, ever co-mingle your business and personal funds!

If you are going to be your own bookkeeper (and in the beginning at least, it should be a very simple process) be sure to balance your bank statement on a monthly basis, preferably within 48 hours of receiving it. This way, it's fairly simple to catch errors and have them resolved by your bank.

With the many computer programs now available, keeping the books is really easy and I find it almost fun since the computer does almost all of the work! If you're thinking about doing it yourself, consider the very popular *Quicken* program—it can make a bookkeeper out of almost anyone, just ask me!

As can happen in even the biggest business, you may from time to time take a check from a customer that bounces. It happens. Don't panic. Simply call the customer and tell them that the check was returned for non-sufficient funds (NSF). If your bank has charged you a fee (and today I don't know of any that don't!) include that amount. Never return the bad check to your customer until you have received a replacement check that has cleared your bank, or you've received a Cashiers Check or Money Order.

If the problem occurs again with the same customer, you may want to do business with them on a cash basis only, get payment up front, or not do business with them at all. From time to time, we all experience problems like this. Just consider it a part of running a business, and rather than take it personally, see the inconvenience as an isolated situation and try not to get upset.

I had a customer call me in somewhat of a panic late one Friday afternoon. He was in desperate need of a resume, as someone had told him of a job that had just opened up and he had to get it to the personnel department by noon on Monday. I'd never dealt with this person before, but he sounded so worried that I agreed to write the resume and have it ready for him on Saturday afternoon.

He showed up, was thrilled with the job I'd done, gave me a check and left. His check bounced, and after redepositing it for the third time, my bank manager called to tell me the account had been closed. Oh, well. I should have asked for cash because I didn't know the man, but I let myself be drawn into his personal predicament. Live and learn.

Business Taxes

As an independent business owner, you will be required to pay your fair share of taxes the same as when you were previously employed. Tax deductions can be advantageous for the home-based business, and careful planning and record-keeping will simplify this part of your typing business. Even though there are many books and now computer based software which enable small business owners to figure their own taxes, it would probably be in your best interest to find and use a competent accountant or tax professional. The combination of your attention to record keeping and a professional's advice will ensure that you pay only as much as you owe.

Businesses pay taxes on gross profits, after all allowable deductions have been taken. If you pay too much in taxes, you're hurting your profit margin. Likewise, if you don't pay enough, you will bring yourself to the attention of the IRS!

To make sure you get the greatest net return on your tax dollars, your tax planning should begin on the first day of each tax year. Don't wait until the end of the year and try to sort out the receipts thrown in a shoebox to figure what you've spent to keep the business running, and what you've been paid by your customers.

You can figure that all ordinary business expenses are tax deductible, but you must have the receipts and records to prove it. Costs associated with advertising, telephone, office supplies and postage are all examples of deductible items. Again, see a professional tax accountant to keep you organized. And, his fees are deductible!

Business Cards - Logo - Letterhead

I'll never forget the first time I ordered my own business cards. It was an exciting moment when I opened the box and saw my name as owner of MY own company! This is a milestone for the new business owner. Your business card says to the world: *Hey Look! I'm In Business! This Is For Real!*

If you are working on a computer with even minimal graphics software, you may want to design your own business cards and letterhead. If not, the task is quite simple using a full-service print shop. All you have to do is look at the hundreds of samples, point to the one you like and say *"I want that one!"* Your printer will do the rest.

If you decide that you'd like to have a *logo* (a piece of artwork or a graphic design that represents your business) on your business cards and stationary, you can pick one already available from the printer, or have one designed. In the beginning though, I wouldn't recommend spending any extra money for this until you're actually making money.

Your business card can be as elaborate or as simple as you desire, but again keep in mind that *economy* is truly the password to new business success. Don't ever feel that you need a four color, glossy business card in order to be successful. In fact, simple and elegant is usually more impressive. Choose a muted, pale color card stock and for this first printing, use only one color ink.

One of the most effective combinations is white cardstock with black ink, possibly dressed up with embossed (raised) letters. Many print shops offer a "Small Business Special" package which includes 500 business cards, 500 letterhead stationary and 500 printed envelopes for a very reasonable price.

Printing is one area where you really need to comparison shop, because most printers are also independent business owners, and while some have been in business for many years with established clients (and higher prices) newer shops may offer bargain pricing to get new business.

There's no need to go to each print shop in person—let your fingers do the walking! Call at least three printers and ask for a quote for the same identical order. Changing even one element such as black plus red ink will change the comparison. Don't be afraid to tell the printer that you're a new business and you're looking for the best price available. He may quote you a lower price just to get your business and hope that in the future you will continue to use his services.

This idea of revealing yourself as a new business owner when shopping for materials, equipment or whatever, has worked quite well for me. It has been my own personal practice to try whenever possible to patronize other small/independent business people. Not only do we have a lot in common, I have been sent a lot of business from the merchants I buy from. In turn, I refer business to them whenever possible.

Chapter 10: Your Working Environment

In today's society, a relatively small (though growing!) percentage of the working population is self-employed. But it wasn't always that way. At the turn of the century in America, almost everyone worked for themselves ..... and usually out of the same location in which they lived. Think about the dressmaker who saw customers in her front parlor, or the doctor who not only made house calls (!), but generally had a room or two on the lower floor of his home where he treated patients.

The concept of working for yourself and doing business from home is not new—it has simply fallen out of vogue since the middle of this century. If you consider that it's only been fifty years since home work was mainstream, it's amazing how many people today still consider it a very strange idea.

The past five years, however, have seen a boom in home-based businesses. Today, there are magazines, trade shows and television documentaries that deal with nothing but issues surrounding the home office. This is good in the sense that people who once chose to work at home often felt isolated and were treated with little respect. Many in the corporate world viewed home-based workers as people who couldn't afford a "real" office, or weren't competent enough to work for a large company.

The benefits of running your word-processing business from your home are many, including tax deductions for mortgage payments, utilities, and home repairs. We've already talked about the money saved now that you don't have to commute, eat out every day, and buy "office" attire. Child care costs should also decrease, and family members will learn how money is really earned by watching what you do to earn it on a daily basis.

But let's not assume that there won't be a period of adjustment for you and everyone else involved. The benefits of working from home are indeed wonderful, but it's also important to make a firm commitment to yourself and your family that work is work! Your ability to perform as a professional will be the determining factor in how successful your home-based business will become. Establishing some ground rules will make the transition easier for everyone.

Developing Self-Discipline

Your commitment to making your typing service a success began at the very moment you decide that working from home is the right career choice for you. It's now up to you to make sure your family and friends understand how important this venture is to you, and that they respect your need for privacy even though you may be literally just a shout away.

It was relatively easy to expect your family to do their fair share when you were leaving for work the same time they were, and arriving home late in the afternoon. Now, as they head off to school and work, there you stand, still in your robe and slippers, sipping another cup of coffee. Their image of you changes, as well as your image of yourself. You're going to have to stand your ground and make them understand that even though you're home during the day, you're still working!

I've discussed this dilemma with many friends who also have home-based offices, and have learned a great deal about how to create and maintain a professional attitude and appearance. Dan, a computer consultant I know, actually leaves his house every morning at 8:30, walks around the block and reenters through the back door, heading straight for his office. This strategy has several benefits: he gets a little morning exercise, he is up and dressed for work (even though it's in shorts and T-shirt) every morning at the same time, and as he goes into his office and turns on the lights, he feels he has actually begun his workday.

My friend Monica is a very successful romance novelist. Her writing involves many hours in front of the computer, not always accomplished between eight a.m. and five p.m. But she is religious in the number of hours she works each day (usually seven) and she allows nothing to keep her from her writing. During that time she never answers the phone (one of the biggest time-wasters for home workers), takes only two fifteen minute breaks, and a thirty minute lunch break. She rewards herself by going to her health club every day and never works on Sunday.

While I admire Monica's dedication and focus, my personality requires a different set of working guidelines (yours probably will too). For one thing, I have to get some fresh air and move around every hour or so. It's not only good for my circulation, but I've incorporated a series of deep breathing exercises which boosts my oxygen intake and really helps clear my head.

Here's my secret: because I continually play soothing background music on tapes while I work, when a tape finishes, I'll have been typing for sixty minutes. The click is my signal to get up and move around. Of course, there are days when I'm not totally focused on work and seem to have a hard time keeping myself at my desk. Find your own system that works.

Without a boss looking over your shoulder every day, it becomes even more important that you get your home office organized and develop a system that will allow you to be in control of your working hours. In the home office environment the old adage time is money, was never more true. You can replace the money if you lose your purse, you can buy a new car if your old one quits running, but you can never make up lost time.

Once the reality of being the boss sets in, it's miraculous how time-conscious the self-employed become. Time efficiency is a challenge, and when you shut off the lights at the end of the day, it's a grand feeling to see what you have accomplished.

One of the greatest tips I've discovered is what I call my "Lost Space," a designated bookcase shelf where things can be dumped until I have the time to sort them out and put them where they're supposed to be. This is a real time-saver because if things are not in the lost space, then they will be put where they belong. The real beauty of this is that I rarely spend any time looking for something. When I think I've lost an important piece of mail that I didn't have time to open yesterday, chances are it's in my lost space. I've also discovered that if I don't pay any attention to the lost space for awhile, most of the items that end up there can be thrown out!

The only people who will be rating your performance are your customers, and about the only time you'll hear from them is when they aren't satisfied with the work you've done for them. Or worse yet, they just won't use you again, and you'll never know why. This can be a little scary for the new entrepreneur, and often overwhelming.

It's going to be entirely up to you to schedule your time, including how many hours and when you work each day, and what projects you choose to work on. There will be no one to blame a late report on. But when you begin to look at this as an incredible challenge instead of a chore, you'll probably discover an area of personal and professional growth just waiting to take off. It's important that you begin to focus on important things, especially those areas of your personal life that may at times take precedence over work. Forget trying to be a perfectionist, as it will slow you down, and remember that too many possessions (especially in the office) can complicate your life. Try to simplify, recalling the old adage that Less is More.

Work Time Productivity

By answering these four simple questions you should begin to feel more confident about your new business:

How many hours will I work each day?   _____

What will my office hours be?   _____

**Will I answer the phone myself
or use an answering machine
or service bureau?**   _____

**Will I see clients in my office
or will I offer pick-up and
delivery service?**   _____

These questions are right-now decisions, and are only the beginning. Your answers will change over time, just as your business changes and grows. But when you're serious about operating a home-based word processing service, you'll find it's easy to stick to your game plan!

Here are ten time-tested ideas for keeping your working hours productive and profitable:

- **Make A Daily "To Do" List Every Morning Or The Night Before.**
- **Give Each Task A Priority Number.**
- **Schedule Time Every Day To Do "Catch Up" Work.**
- **Set Deadlines In Writing.**
- **Keep A Master Calendar Where You Can Always See It.**
- **Let The Answering Machine Pick Up Phone Calls.**
- **Keep A Notepad At Hand For Things You Think Of To Do.**
- **Buy And Use Your Day-Planner Book Religiously.**
- **Do Office Housekeeping & Filing Once A Week**
- **Remember What You Charge Per Hour. If You're Not Working Smart—You're Lo$Ing Money!**

Creating Your Work Space

It's going to be very important to you, your family, and especially your customers that the image you project is one of absolute professionalism. If you don't make an immediate effort to define your office conditions, working hours, and communication procedures, it will be next to impossible to be taken seriously.

In my writing and publishing ventures I almost always use home-based typesetters, proofreaders and graphics people. But I'll tell you right off, a screaming child in the background does nothing to boost my confidence in a graphic designer that I've just handed a $5,000 order to! This is not to say that the person isn't capable of doing excellent work, or that she won't bring the job in on time, it's just that first impressions are so vitally important to those of us whose usual office attire is sweat pants!

Whether you set up your home office in a spare bedroom, the basement or attic, the most valuable item your new office will have is a door. I can't stress enough the importance of choosing an area that is totally separate from the rest of your personal life. There was a time when my writing was going so slowly (meaning I couldn't sell a vowel!) that financial neces-

sity forced my family of four into a two bedroom duplex. Granted, my bedroom was a large as most apartments are today and had the most magnificent oak tree outside—but the problem was where to locate my typewriter (I wasn't a computer nut back then).

Since my bedroom had a door, and more than enough room for my desk and a file cabinet, that's where I worked. All was fine until it came time to go to bed. I had a TV at the foot of the bed, and just behind it sat my desk piled with papers, stacks of research materials, open books and notes taped to everything. As I lay in bed pretending to watch the eleven o'clock news, my eyes were magnetized by my "office" and all I could think of was work! I couldn't ever relax enough to go to sleep.

My wonderful husband corrected the situation after months of me crawling out of bed at one a.m. to make notes or read at my desk. He bought me a four bedroom house! I've had a separate office (with a door) ever since.

Try to remember when setting up your office that not only are you creating an environment that will stimulate and encourage you to do your best work, you are also making a statement about who you are professionally. Although office clutter overtakes all of us at one time or another, spend some time each week on aesthetics and organizational chores.

Learn to work smarter by making a conscious effort to control your working environment and the ensuing profit making activities will guarantee your business success. You may operate your typing business on a strictly pick-up and delivery basis, but periodically look around your office and ask yourself how it would look to your best client if he/she were to just drop by unexpectedly!

Ideally your office will provide enough room to not only work, but to move about comfortably. I have my Great Aunt Yetta's rocking chair in my office. A beautiful, hand-carved mahogany masterpiece brought to this country from Russia by her father, it has been the most fought-over family heirloom. I can just hear my cousins saying "She keeps it hidden in that office, for Pete's sake!" Hidden? No way.

When I run out of things to write about, I make a cup of tea and sit in that chair and stare out the window. It soothes me. It connects me to a time long ago when women like me spent their lives cooking and cleaning, and taking care of everyone around them. That's all they were allowed to do. I'm soon counting my blessings and am back to work.

So what does the well equipped home office look like? That's entirely up to you. But once you've installed the necessities: desk, chair (the absolute best you can afford!), file cabinets, lighting, and storage compartments, the more energy you put into making your office a place you really enjoy being, the easier it will be to begin each day.

A window for lots of fresh air was the first priority for me. Having spent years in unventilated offices breathing old, stale air, my own private window was at the very top of my list. Other niceties include carpeting and lots of plants to purify the air. My walls are filled with posters, awards, family art and photos. This is truly my space, just as your office will be yours. Don't make the mistake of thinking you need to furnish your office with the sterile look of today's high-tech environments. That's one of the reasons you're in business for yourself, remember!

Mary, another local writer that I call for inspiration from time to time, has created an aura of Old World elegance in her home office. She has the most beautiful dark cherry wood desk and credenza (salvaged from a law firm renovation) that she paid $100 for, total. Her mother gave her an antique oriental rug in shades of gold and burgundy (the worn spots are hidden by potted ferns). She moved two very old and worn leather chairs from her husband's den under her office window, and often invites the people she's interviewing to come for the afternoon.

Start creating your home office ambiance by canvassing the garages and attics of friends, neighbors and relatives. Old desks are usually hidden beneath piles of junk. When I needed additional desk space, I only had to take a walk to my own garage. There was a massive desk that had been left (at my husband's request) by the people we bought the house from. All it needed was a good cleaning and some touch-up work and I now have an entire desk on which I can pile more things!

Take that still-life that's been hanging in your dining room forever (you love it - everyone else hates it), and hang it in your new office. It's not money that creates the best home office, it's what makes you feel inspired, creative, and ready to tackle each new day with joy and enthusiasm. Here are some great tricks I've learned from other home workers:

- **Carpeting mutes the clatter of telephones & printers**
- **Drapes ensure privacy and security**
- **Files mounted on walls save work space**
- **Music provides company and soothes the soul**
- **Mirrors reflect your commitment to success**
- **Answering machines save time and money**

The 80/20 Rule

The Italian economist Pareto had a foolproof theory named after him, and what he basically discovered was that 80% of your business will come from 20% of your clients. It's the old 80/20 rule that salespeople live by. For the home-based typist this can also be translated to mean:

20% Of Your Business Efforts Will Generate

80% Of Your Income

But before you can get out there and drum up the business, you need the right equipment. See the next chapter for a detailed discussion of how to set up shop!

Chapter 11: Choosing Your Equipment

Having been a self-employed writer (on and off) for the last twenty years, I've learned some very important, and hard lessons about the tools of my trade. Just as a carpenter can't build a house without the right tools, operating a home-based typing business also requires some specific equipment. But don't quit reading now, afraid that I'm going to tell you that you must run out and bury yourself in mega-debt to get this business up and running!

The truth is, you need something to type on. It must be reliable, comfortable to your touch, and able to deliver the finished product that you guarantee your customers. Whether for you this means an IBM Correcting Selectric typewriter, or a state of the art personal computing system with all the bells and whistles, this decision is yours ..... and your budget's.

When I finally realized that all I ever really wanted to do was be a writer, I was typing my heart out on a little Smith Corona portable typewriter. This baby was one of the first-ever electric portables and weighed only nine pounds. My husband gave it to me as a birthday gift, but prior to that I had always typed on an old government issue manual clunker that my father had bought at a surplus auction when I was about eight years old. Hey, it made letters on the page, and when I did get that first electric, my typing speed was about 65 words per minute. I had to practice slowing my fingers down to keep from making so many mistakes!

Today, I'm what's considered a Macintosh computer junkie—I'm on my third system. We moved into our dream home last year, and while sorting and cleaning I came across a box that contained many of my first manuscripts, all churned out on that little Smith Corona. I held them lovingly, they were like my babies who are also now grown and gone. I looked at those typed pages and marveled at the advances in technology that now make my writing working life so simple. But the point I'd like to make is ..... if I had to, I could still work on an electric typewriter. So can you if that's what you have to do.

Before we get too involved in the pros and cons of typewriters, word processors, computers and the like, let's take a moment to investigate some of the other equipment you'll need to launch your home typing business.

Telephone Options

Your telephone is your link to the world ..... your customers ..... your success. In the initial stages of setting up shop, if your budget is tight, use your home phone for your business too. It's probably wise to check with your local telephone company to find out what their policy is.

In some localities, you only need to get a business phone number if you want a listing in the Yellow pages. With the recent competition in phone services, there are now so many options available that you will want to call the Business Office of your phone company to find out exactly what they can do for you.

One of the biggest problems for the home-based business is family members tying up the line with personal calls, or answering the phone in an unprofessional manner that could end up costing you business. My friend Jason is a single father and a home-based architectural consultant who solved this problem by teaching his teenage son how to properly answer the phone for business and take messages, and by restricting his use of the phone for personal calls to after 5 p.m.

I recently subscribed to an offer I saw on one of those infomercials and still can't believe how technology has moved into the home. Through my phone company (GTE) I now have:

- Call Forwarding
- An entirely separate phone number for my business
- Four voice mail boxes

• No more Call Waiting because the voice mail now takes messages while I'm talking to someone else.

I can even retrieve and save the messages I want to keep and erase everything else. With this "Smart Secretary" feature, I can program appointments and important dates up to one year in advance, and then my phone rings that morning to tell me that my dog needs to go to the veterinarian for her shots at two o'clock that afternoon! All this for $7.95 (plus the usual monthly phone charges) per month! These are sophisticated features that many big businesses don't even have yet!

If you don't have this type of service in your area yet, there are still lots of options for a home-based business. The answering machine is still another great solution and probably the least expensive option, offering twenty-four hour dependability and a host of features that make your work life manageable.

If you decide an answering machine is the way to go, try to get one that allows you to call from anywhere and retrieve your messages and also has a "time stamp" feature that will tell you what time the caller called. One of my own rules when I'm writing is to only answer the phone between three and five p.m. The rest of the day, I'll let my calls be picked up on Voice Mail and when I take a break, I'll listen to my calls. If it's something urgent, I can call right back, otherwise I try to return all calls late in the afternoon when I'm usually tired of writing anyway and have time to chat.

You'd be wise to remember that people still want to talk to a human being, and most of us are fed up with electronic switchboards that force you to punch in a zillion numbers only to be disconnected. If you can, answer the phone yourself, but if your customers must leave a message on your answering machine, make it simple for them. Record your outgoing message to sound as warm as possible, but still professional. Maybe ask your sister who's a radio announcer to record your message. Keep it simple and brief:

"Hello. This is Mary Jones Typing Service. Please leave a message and I'll call you back as soon as I'm available."

Another possibility is using a professional answering service, the kind that uses live operators to answer your calls. This type of service, however, will add another expense to your new business start-up costs (not recommended), and many people have complained about incomplete or incorrect messages.

The Fax Machine

The modern Fax machine is no longer something to put on your wish list for your new office, it's become almost a necessity. Just ask me. My three year old Fax died a slow and painful death after ninety mile an hour winds buffeted my hilltop for what seemed an eternity. The resulting brownout (we never actually lost power, it was just barely flickering) proved lethal to my trusted friend. Since that fateful day, I think every person I've spoken to on the phone has said, "Just *Fax it over to me.*" Oh, if only I could!

Considering that the prices for Fax machines have been cut in half in the last few years, they're a good investment. I recently saw one of the lower end Fax machines advertised for less than $300! A Fax machine will instantly make your business appear more credible (what large business doesn't have a Fax number?), can save hours of pick up and delivery time, and allows you to send and receive information from clients that could otherwise be delayed by playing the proverbial phone tag.

For proofing the final typed version of anything, there's nothing like being able to sent it directly to your client by Fax, and have it returned with corrections or approval in a matter of hours. This type of routine correspondence used to take days if it were done locally, longer if documents had to be sent by mail.

If you're not quite ready to invest in this equipment, don't despair. There are many local Fax service bureaus that can provide you with everything you need to join the Fax revolution. You should carefully compare the prices these outlets charge (usually by the page) and also make sure that they will call you immediately upon receipt of your incoming Fax. Try these types of business to handle your Fax needs:

- Copy Centers   • Libraries   • Office Supply

- Mail Service Centers   • Quick Print

Since my Fax machine bit the dust I've been using my neighborhood MAILBOXES, ETC. franchise for all my Fax needs, and will continue to do so until I have the time to comparison shop for a new Fax. It's a bit on the expensive side this way, but they're wonderful about calling me when something comes in, and they even delivered an urgent Fax to my house one day when I was in a panic.

To comparison shop intelligently if you've decided you can't live without a Fax machine, here are the three most important things you should know:

• You can save money by using the same telephone line for both phone and fax.

• Some machines can also double as a telephone answering machine and a photocopier.

• Baud refers to how fast information can be sent. 9600 baud is almost twice as fast as 4800 baud.

Do I Really Need A Copy Machine?

Maybe yes ..... maybe no! This is one of those tough questions. If you plan to type resumes and cover letters, and your client needs 25 copies of each on fancy parchment paper, then the answer might be yes. However, a resume service where I live got around this by stressing the composition and formatting of the resume instead of number of copies. They gave the client a master copy and told them it would be cheaper to go directly to a copy shop and have additional copies made as they were needed.

Unless you plan to utilize this major piece of equipment on a daily basis, *and* have customers already lined up that you know will require multiple copies of the documents you will produce for them, don't spend your

money on a copy machine in the beginning. There are too many other ways to solve the problem of multiple copies, for a lot less money.

Back to my local Mailboxes, Etc., a very enterprising young couple who offer a half price copy special every Saturday. I can copy anything I want for a nickel per page, and that's on *their* fancy colored paper! I usually try and save up all of my copying work for that day, but even if I need 100 copies of something on Wednesday, it's still only seven cents a copy.

I've also adopted that resume service's policy, and usually ask my publisher or editor to make the copies they need from the original manuscript that I send. They already have the equipment on hand, and the manpower to do the job.

I must also mention Kinko's Copy Centers here, because for the independent, home-based entrepreneur they provide many different services that used to be available only to very large companies. It would be well worth your while to find one close to your home and spend some time exploring their store. Introduce yourself to one of the managers as a new home-based typing service and let them show you all the things they can do for you. Whether it's Faxing documents, collating and printing a thousand copies of a report, or helping you with designing a brochure you've been hired to put together, this place really does it all. And ..... they will pick up and deliver!

Typewriter, Word Processor or Computer?

Since the main product you will be selling is your typing ability, the question of what equipment you will work on is probably the most important you will face. As I said before, there is absolutely no reason why you can't begin your word processing business with an electric typewriter, and if you don't have one already, getting one is not at all difficult.

If your start-up funds are limited, ask family members, friends, and co-workers if they, or anyone they know might have an electric typewriter they're not using. You should also watch for office equipment auctions at your local university or school district. Most office supply stores (check your Yellow Pages) refurbish and sell used typewriters. Make friends with the owner and let him know what you're looking for and approximately how much you can spend.

Also be sure to regularly check the classified ads in your local newspaper for used office equipment. I desperately needed additional filing cabinets for my home office, but couldn't justify the cost of new ones. I found exactly what I had been looking for in the newspaper when a bank closed one of its branches and sold off the office equipment. My four drawer, locking fireproof file cabinets (I bought two) cost me a total of $28!

If you're already doing word processing on a computer and have decided to implement those skills into your new typing service, the question then arises, should I buy a dedicated word processor or a computer and printer? What's the difference?

What Is A Dedicated Word Processor?

And dedicated to what, you wonder? You? Well, not exactly. Both personal computers and dedicated word processors are in fact *computers*, but there are some big differences. Understanding these differences will help you make the right choice.

A dedicated word processor is exactly what the name implies, a system dedicated to doing one job: word processing. Because of this, dedicated word processors really shine in helping you create and edit text. They usually resemble a computer in appearance, although a few of the more simple ones look like a typewriter with a small screen.

The computer-based word processing system is different in that it is based around a microcomputer, more commonly referred to as a personal computer, or PC. It is distinguished from a dedicated word processor by the fact that it is not designed to do just one job, but can be used to do many different things depending on the type of software running on it. Here are some of the reasons many typing services choose a dedicated word processor over a complete computer system:

- **Less Expensive Than A Computer**
- **Easier To Learn**
- **More Portable Than A Computer**

On the other hand, choosing a personal computer gives you a larger range of options including your choice of literally hundreds of software programs that could help you upgrade the services you offer your customers. Another factor to consider is that the resale value of a dedicated word processor is usually well below that of a PC—but then the initial investment is not as great either.

When my trusty old Smith Corona finally flung its last semicolon onto the page, I panicked. Already several years behind the computer revolution, I was faced with the terrifying prospect of learning what all the fuss was about, doing the necessary homework to make a rational purchase, and figuring out how to pay for what I thought would be akin to my mortgage.

I worried needlessly. Since I was solvent enough to have a Sears charge account, I gathered up my courage and headed down to where America shops. The first salesperson I talked to knew even less than I did about the computer revolution, so I politely asked if he would please find someone who could explain the difference between a dot matrix and laser quality printer. (I borrowed those terms from an article I was researching!)

The department manager appeared, plastic pocket protector and all. I was relieved. I told him of my dilemma, my skill level, my fear of becoming a computer nerd and about my very limited budget. After asking me all kinds of questions about what exactly I used my typewriter for, he gently led me over to a row of foreign looking machines and introduced me to the modern dedicated word processor.

It was love at first sight! The little screen, the detachable keyboard ..... I guess I really did want to join the computer revolution, I just needed someone to hold my hand. To make this story short, I bought one of the very first Brother Word Processors, on sale for $449.00. I charged it to my account, bought a box of 3 1/2 inch floppy disks, and headed for home.

This type of equipment requires little more than plugging it in, because it comes with a tutorial (teaching) disk that you just pop into the machine and it tells you how everything works! I was up and running having typed my first document within three hours, and have never looked back. I worked on that Brother every day for almost six years without a moment's trouble.

Today's dedicated word processors are vastly improved, with greater storage (also known as memory) capacity and faster processing speed. Many machines now have additional software available that will do simple bookkeeping and accounting functions. I just saw an ad last week for a new Smith Corona Word Processor that included a 12" EGA monitor (my old one was only 6"), spreadsheet software, built in 75,000 word spell-checker and 96,000 word thesaurus. The price ..... $299! Such a deal!

If you are considering investing in a dedicated word processor, here are some of the features you will want to make sure the system offers:

- **Search And Replace**
- **File Merge And Write**
- **Insert - Overwrite**

- **Word Wrap**
- **Full Cursor Movement**
- **Screen Or Line Editing**
- **Formatting Commands**
- **Variable Tab Settings**
- **Copy Block Movement**
- **Page And Line Number Status**
- **Automatic Headers And Footers**
- **Service And Warranty Guarantee**

One of the most important and useful features both dedicated word processors and software based PC's offer is the spell checker. This incredible option is a vital element in all word processing operations as it can automate the critical mechanical process of proofreading your typed documents.

A spell checker operates by scanning words in the document and then comparing them with a built-in dictionary file. If there is a mistake, the spell checker highlights the word and makes the correction. When looking at the system, a good spell checker should include a dictionary of at least 100,000 words. It should also offer you the option of adding words, names, special nouns, etc. to the dictionary as you need to. Most spell checkers also offer a preview function which allows you to see an incorrect word before any changes are made. If you plan to do a lot of work in the legal field, some spell checkers include lists of technical words related specifically to that field.

Don't be shy about taking a list of questions with you when you comparison shop for any type of equipment. If the salesperson is hesitant, or appears uninterested in answering your questions fully, find another place that will become your ally, and where you can go for help and information in the future.

For just about any type of equipment you may need for your business, it may be in your best interest to consider leasing. If you don't have the cash available, have reasonably good credit, and especially if you are still employed, you may be able to lease your equipment through the manufacturer. Many manufacturers even offer lease-to-purchase plans, where you make a monthly payment towards the equipment, then at a pre-agreed time, you have the option of purchasing, with some or possibly all of your payments going towards the purchase price.

A dedicated word processor is an ideal choice for your typing business and will easily accomplish the following activities:

- Letters
- Memos
- Newsletters
- Resumes
- Brochures

- Books
- Reports
- Articles
- Press Releases
- And More!

So You've Decided To Buy A Computer

Congratulations! This will probably be the most terrifying and exciting decision concerning your new venture that you'll have to make. Investing in computer hardware and software can be a challenging task, but don't be scared off by those who act like they know everything and you know nothing. With a little research and by asking a lot of questions, you too will become familiar with the new generation of computers and all the things that they can do for you.

Before you decide to buy any type of equipment, here are five rules you need to remember:

- Know How Much You Can Afford
- Be Skeptical Of All Salespeople
- Comparison Shop At Least Three Stores
- Get All Promises And Warranties In Writing
- Read The Instructions Before You Buy

One of the most helpful publications on the market for home-based entrepreneurs is *Home Office Computing* (see Resources at the end of this book). This monthly magazine is slick, well written, and offers the most complete information I've found on what's hot (and not!) for people who run their business out of their home. Their monthly reviews and comments on computer stuff are sometimes over my head, but I've learned so much from reading this magazine, I can't recommend it enough.

My friend John is absolutely brilliant when it comes to computers. Having worked for the government and aerospace industry for many years, he now runs a home-based computer consulting business. When it was time for me to upgrade my own equipment (I finally outgrew my dedicated word processor) he was of course, the first person I called. We began a love-hate phone relationship that has lasted to this day!

John is a dyed-in-the-wool IBM person, and even though he tried his best, I ended up buying an Apple Macintosh system. Why? Because at the time, the Mac was so much simpler to use. In the last few years however, IBM has incorporated what's called Windows which makes it (almost) as user friendly. What's really exciting is that if you listen to the computer wizards, it won't be long before most software will work on both IBM and Mac platforms.

While I'm no computer expert, and have no desire to become one, the best advice I can give you is to find one! I have a Mac tutor (he used to be a paramedic and now also is a home-based entrepreneur) who charges me a very reasonable hourly rate for phone consultations if I can't figure out how to do something, or get in trouble, or need information about new software. It's well worth the price (and it's tax deductible), but what's even better is that we've worked out a trade agreement where I create his flyers and marketing materials and he teaches me how to make the best use of my computer.

The advice another writer gave me, which I'd like to pass on to you, is to find yourself a computer junkie, tell them what you want your computer system to do for you, and then let them figure it all out. That's pretty much what I've done. The industry changes so quickly, that if I were to try and keep up with all the new information, I'd have no time to write, and then I'd have no business!

A Gold Mine For You: Computer Discount Magazines

If you're leaning towards purchasing a PC or Macintosh computer, but the price still has you hesitating, then check out the great deals available to you in computer discount magazines. Here are three major vendors that offer exceptional deals on PC and Macintosh computers and other products:

PC & MacConnection, 800-800-1111 (Both PC and Mac products)
MacMall, 800-222-2808 (Mac products only)
MacWarehouse, 800-255-6227 (Mac products only)

Call the 800 numbers to receive your free catalog from each of these vendors. MacWarehouse and PC & MacConnection offer overnight delivery of any item by Federal Express for just $3. (MacMall has the same offer, but with a weight limit of 10 lbs.)

Another advantage of buying your equipment from these vendors is you can avoid paying state sales tax. In other words, if you don't live in the state where they are located, you don't have to pay sales tax! Now, when you're buying a big-ticket item like a computer or a printer, that can mean substantial savings. Here's the breakdown of the vendors by sales tax:

PC & MacConnection: only Ohio residents pay sales tax.
MacMall: only California residents pay sales tax.
MacWarehouse: only Connecticut, New Jersey, and Ohio residents pay sales tax.

I have personally bought a $1500 laser printer from MacConnection—on the advice of my computer adviser—and the service was everything promised. Overnight delivery for $3 and no sales tax! And I've never had a problem with this printer.

Another important note about these catalogs is that many more products are available than are listed. For example, PC & MacConnection lists only 1,000 products in their catalog, but they carry over 20,000 products! So it pays to call the 800 number and ask, even if you don't see it in the catalog.

A Final Note

Yes, it's important to know as much as you need to about the equipment you use, but don't let it rule your life. You don't need to know how the fuel injection system works in your car to drive it. Likewise, you don't have to know everything about your computer to get Dr. Martin's article on osteoporosis typed by the deadline!

Chapter 12: Advertising, Marketing and Public Relations

Three very separate components crucial to the success of your business are advertising, marketing and public relations. While many feel that because these things are usually lumped together they are the same, make no mistake—advertising is different from marketing, and public relations is yet another part of selling your services. Let's simplify the confusion by defining what each element does and how it's accomplished. Webster's gives us the following definitions:

• **(ad~ver~tis~ing)** — *printed or spoken matter, to warn, call attention to; to tell people about or praise, as through newspapers, radio, etc., usually so as to get them to buy.*

• **(mar~ket~ing)** — *to sell, to offer for sale, to deal in a market, that can be sold, a demand for.*

• **(pub~lic re~la~tions)** — *the process of obtaining and maintaining public awareness, understanding and support; informing the public through publicity, attempt to create favorable opinion.*

These three functions create the foundation for telling about and selling your services. Accept right now that promoting your word processing business will be something that you do almost every minute of every day. Having a roster of happy clients is wonderful, but never forget that you must always be sowing the seeds to keep your stable full. The best way to guarantee the long-term success of your word processing business is to commit a portion of each working day to marketing or promoting your services.

Is there any great mystery or secret to creating your own successful marketing program? Not really, but there are things you can do that don't cost an arm and a leg that will speed up the process of getting clients on board and $$$ coming in. Do you need to hire an advertising agency? No, and you probably couldn't afford one anyway! *So what does marketing your typing service really involve?*

- **Getting The Word Out**
- **Showing Why Your Service Is Superior**
- **Reminding Your Customers About Your Services Often**
- **Keeping Your Business Visible**
- **Getting Customer Referrals**
- **Creating A Memorable Image**

One of the true joys of owning and operating your home-based typing service is learning to do things you've probably never had to do before. If your work experience has been limited to a specific field, or job classification, you've probably had little exposure to writing advertising copy, or standing up in front of a group of women professionals telling them what you do.

The personal and professional growth that come from being "THE BOSS" is an added bonus. Take advantage of the fact that you can and will be required to do many things to promote your new business that you've never done before. The more often you put yourself into new learning situations, the more you'll grow and the more confident you'll become.

One of the most important things you can do immediately for yourself and your new business is to join your local Chamber of Commerce. If you're not familiar with this organization, all you really need to know is that its sole purpose is to support and encourage small local business people like yourself.

If you can't afford the membership fee at first, attend the meetings and mixers as a guest until you can. Talk to either the Chamber President or Executive Director about paying your membership fee in installments. Your local Chamber of Commerce is the quickest way to get yourself known to other business people who can and will use your services. In return, your Chamber of Commerce needs your help in chairing committees, staffing and other volunteer capacities.

The entire organization works on a volunteer basis, with the exception of the Executive Director and perhaps office staff that actually run the Chamber office. There are many other networking organizations that can help you promote your new business and we'll talk about the networking concept later in this chapter.

But right now, pick up the phone, call your Chamber of Commerce, introduce yourself and your business and ask them to send you a new member packet—*it's free!*

Advertising

If you've never had any experience in buying, selling or creating advertising, don't worry. Having worked as an Ad Director in the newspaper industry for *(too)* many years, the most important ingredient in any advertising campaign is: *common sense.*

So far you've been brave enough to envision the joys and benefits of working for yourself, so don't be intimidated because you haven't mastered every skill you'll need in your new business. I would suggest heading to your local library and checking out every book they have which covers the topic *"How To Advertise and Promote Your Small Business."* I'm not quoting any exact title here, I only know there are many books now available that deal with this subject. Read everything you can find *before* you spend a dime!

Here are some fancy terms advertising people use that you should probably know, and will eventually understand how they affect your business.

• **Demographics** are the vital statistics (age, income, education, etc.) of a targeted group of prospective customers.

• **Reach** refers to the number of people potentially exposed to your advertising message, usually expressed as a percentage of the total marketplace.

• **Frequency** is the number of times the people you reach are exposed to your advertising message.

• **Cost Per Thousand (CPM)** is a formula used to compare similar print media by determining which publications best reach your target audience for the lowest cost.

Over the years I, like many small business people, have spent a lot of money on advertising, marketing and promotions. Some have cost very little and been enormously successful, others almost bankrupt me and brought no new business. There are no hard and fast rules for promoting your new business except be very cautious when writing a check! Money spent foolishly on untested advertising schemes will almost always end in failure.

Even with many years of experience in the advertising field, I recently managed to break every rule I've ever learned. I spent big bucks on advertising and promoting a writing seminar that my market research indicated would draw at least one hundred people. I rented a large room at a local hotel and had it set up for that number. I didn't panic when only twenty had preregistered the day before the seminar. *"They'll show up at the door ....."* I rationalized.

They didn't. And in spite of heavy newspaper advertising, press releases, radio spots and interviews, only nineteen people showed up. I lost my proverbial shirt. The moral: do your homework, plan your advertising campaign—*and if you're lucky, it might just work!*

Print Advertising

Print advertising—that is, advertising in newspapers, magazines, and other printed publications—is one of the best ways to reach *any* audience. I'm a big fan of Classified Advertising for small, service-oriented businesses. Newspaper advertising offers many advantages to the small business:

- **Exposes your message to a large audience**
- **Reaches very specific target segments**
- **Creates a visible, tangible, reality-based message**
- **Offers coupon opportunities**
- **Requires minimum lead time**

Most newspapers have a Business & Service directory that offers weekly or daily advertising exposure for a very nominal rate. They usually charge by the line so that if the line rate is $9.00 and you run a three line ad, the cost for the ad is $27.00. If you decide to try this type of advertising, give your service directory ad at least a thirty-day trial period, as research has proven that it takes repeated exposure for any type of advertising to be effective. *(Remember with any advertising that you do to always "source" your new clients. That means asking them directly how they heard about you.)*

Weekly community shoppers (also known as throwaways), college newspapers, and Chamber of Commerce monthly publications are all cost effective forms of print advertising. The beauty of spending your advertising dollars on print is that prospective customers who might not need your service at the moment can always tear your ad out of the paper and save it for future use.

Newspaper advertising results are also very easy to track, so you know exactly how many people call from the ad and if it is worth the cost to continue running it. For a home-based word processing business, I wouldn't suggest spending money on display advertising because it's usually very expensive. Let's look at how the cost is figured.

Say the column inch rate = $10.00 per column inch (1 column wide X 1 inch deep). An ad that is 2 columns wide X 2 inches deep = 4 column inches. Four column inches X $10.00 = $40.00. *That's how much it will cost you each and every time your ad runs!!!*

Most newspapers will try and get you to sign some sort of contract, committing you to a specific number of lines (classified) or inches (display) per month or year. Until your business is well established, don't sign anything. Use what's known as an "Open Rate" and advertise only when and where you need to.

If your ad placed in the Business Directory continually brings in new business and phone calls, then it might be time to talk to your advertising representative at the newspaper about signing a contract. It *could* save you some money.

The Yellow Pages

We know that Yellow Pages (I use the term to refer to all types of telephone directory advertising) advertising works because it's been around forever, and the books just keep getting bigger and bigger! Is it right for your home-based typing business? It may very well be, but in the beginning it will probably be too expensive, and can also complicate the issue of using your home phone number to list your business.

As we discussed in Chapter Six, some phone companies restrict the use of personal numbers. To list your business in the Yellow Pages, you will probably have to install a business phone line. Your best bet is to call the business office of your phone company and find out the procedure.

To be on the conservative side, I would suggest that you wait until your business has been established at least one year before you commit to a listing in the Yellow Pages. The cost of Yellow Pages advertising is quite high, and should you fail to make your monthly payment as agreed, the phone company *could* disconnect your phone. *No phone ..... no business!*

When you decide it may be time to investigate Yellow Pages advertising, call the phone company and ask to see a representative. Chances are, a simple line listing will be more than adequate (and affordable), but you may want a display ad. Just remember, the representative is a *salesperson ....* who probably gets paid on a commission basis. Don't be pressured into buying more advertising than you need, or can afford.

Flyers, Newsletters and Brochures

Promotional literature that you design yourself will be one of the most useful and cost effective ways to tell the world about your business. The real beauty of this type of advertising is the ability to change your message to suit the audience you're trying to capture.

Once you've written your basic mission statement (just a fancy term for what your business actually does) it's a fairly simple process to customize the marketing materials to suit that target. This basic "one sheet" can also be used to offer discounts, coupons, and other promotions designed strictly to generate new business, or track current customer trends.

Getting back to my ill-fated writing seminar, had I simply relied on the 8 1/2 x 11" flyer I designed and produced on my Mac, instead of spending huge amounts of money on newspaper display advertising, I would have at least broken even! I used a preprinted type of artwork available through a mail order company called Idea Art, went to my local quick print shop and had 1,000 flyers printed. At 7¢ apiece on brightly colored stock, the entire promotion cost less than $75.00.

I blanketed my local community, leaving copies of the flyer in all bookstores, libraries, community centers, anyplace I thought would-be writers might gather. I also posted the flyers on every bulletin board and grocery store kiosk in town. After hand distributing and posting, I used the remainder of the flyers for a direct mail campaign and enclosed my business card with each piece. Direct mail can be a very effective way of getting your business known, but it can also be costly and time consuming.

Small, specifically targeted mailings tend to be most effective for independent businesses, and remember to always include your business card. Main Street Medical Group may not need your service at the moment they receive your direct mailed flyer, but will most likely add your business card to the file containing future typing needs.

How else can you use a promotional flyer? I sent the writing seminar flyer to every newspaper in the area, and received two very nice write-ups about not only the upcoming seminar, but also about my copywriting services as well. Free advertising! Having your promotional flyer at your fingertips will also help you with your daily marketing efforts.

Every morning as I read the newspaper, I pull out the Fictitious Business Name Statements (the ones you need to file if you do business under a name other than your own). Those legal notices list the name(s) of the owner and the address of both the business and the person filing the notice. I send every new business a flyer and one of my cards and then add the name to my own card file with the date I sent the information. At the end of thirty days, I call the operator for directory assistance and after getting the phone number of the new business, I do a follow-up call to introduce myself and my services.

I also make good use of the daily business section following the same procedure, and I send my flyer to all businesses regarding their personnel promotions, new contracts or awards presented. Anytime I find the name of someone I think could use my services, I send them a promotional flyer or letter and business card. I'm amazed at the number of people I've met at business functions who remember me, even though we've never met!

This very same concept works using the Help Wanted section in the classifieds. I read them every day, and whenever a business runs an ad looking for a person to do the type of work I do independently, I send them a letter offering my services on a freelance basis, plus my business card.

What's the difference between a flyer, a brochure and a newsletter? Basically the cost! Flyers are an inexpensive way to reach a lot of people with your message. A brochure is the big brother to the flyer, is generally printed on higher quality card stock, with a relatively generic message that can be used for all of your marketing efforts. The brochures I have now are quite slick looking since I hired a graphic artist to create the three fold design and artwork (*I wrote the copy of course!*). This is not my everyday promo-

tional literature and because of the cost involved, I only send this brochure to clients I have already spoken to, and believe will become active clients.

Do you need a newsletter? As your business grows and develops, this type of marketing may become useful. Once you have an active customer base (say 10-50 clients) you may find a monthly or quarterly newsletter very helpful in keeping your name in front of them. Your newsletter can be used to let your clients know about new services you are offering, congratulations on any awards or big contracts, new clients who have signed on with you, etc.

A local interior design consultant has me write the copy for her quarterly newsletter and always includes a coupon for a free consultation. She says it's the only advertising she does, mailing it to about one hundred customers and new contacts four times a year. She says the coupon usually brings ten to twenty phone inquiries.

Radio & Cable Television Advertising

Electronic media is often considered too sophisticated and expensive for most small, independent businesses. But this is not always the case if your market area is small and buying air time is within your budget. Although print advertising can offer more proven results (customers walk in with coupon in hand) it doesn't have the far reaching effectiveness of radio's "top of mind" penetration. Radio advertising can give you:

- **High frequency due to low out-of-pocket costs**
- **Well targeted reach depending on the station format**
- **On-air promotional opportunities**
- **Flexibility: you can change your message easily**

Using your precious advertising dollars on radio or TV to promote your typing service may be something you want to explore once your business is fairly well known, but trying to create an awareness in the marketplace for a new business would probably be a wasted effort. *Unless .....*

You plan on generating a good percentage of your business from your local college community, including students and professors. Then it might be worthwhile to contact those schools to see if they have a student-run radio or TV station. Because these stations are a part of the curriculum, are run by students, and most likely are subsidized by the school, advertising rates may be well within your budget. I found a way to use radio to promote my writing seminar—and even though attendance was not great, I can't tell you how many people told me they heard about it on the radio!

The main reason I decided to spend the money was because I managed to get two separate radio stations to interview me on the air prior to the seminar, and, they offered me really low spots rate for the commercials. Remember though, I've worked in advertising for years and know how to negotiate. People that sell "air" time are sophisticated and may easily overwhelm you with statistics and a convincing sales pitch. Make sure you have enough information *and money* before you begin talking to media reps!

While cable television advertising can be inexpensive in some localities and is a fairly good way to get your name recognized in your community, the greatest cost factor comes in producing the 30 or 60 second "spot." If your local cable company has a community calendar or bulletin board on the air, you may want to place your ad on it.

These programs usually consist of stationary ads that include a printed message and a phone number. Call your local cable company to find out if this type of advertising would work for you. Remember to keep your overall advertising budget in mind, and if you decide to try it, give it at least a thirty day trial period.

Networking

For the new word processing business, networking, or word-of-mouth promotion, will probably be the most successful and definitely the most cost effective. Some of the quickest ways to get your business off the ground are:

- **Make Your Former Boss Your First Client**
- **Call Your Competition And Ask For Any Overflow Work They Can't Handle**
- **Use Contacts From Your Former Job As References**

- **Check The Classified Ads For Jobs You Could Do, Call And Sell Your Services**
- **Give Your Business Card To Everyone**
- **Offer A "Bird-Dog" Fee To Anyone Who Sends You A Client That Results In Work**

One of the most important things you'll need to do not only as your business gets off the ground, but as a continuous part of your marketing effort, will be to join business and professional organizations and regularly attend their meetings. When you own your own business, remember: *every person that you come into contact with becomes a potential customer!*

It's important to get in the habit of always carrying your business cards with you, and don't be shy about handing them out. My friend Jeannie spent years as a secretary, making very little money and earning even less respect. On a dare, she decided to go to work on her uncle's car lot as a salesperson. She attended every sales seminar that was offered, paid close attention to the way the seasoned salesmen worked their customers, and within a year had tripled her income!

Jeannie told me about a sales rally she once attended where the speaker explained that whenever he was at a sports event with a large crowd, he took along a box of 1,000 business cards. Every time the fans stood up to cheer, he stood up too and threw handfuls of his business cards!

HOT TIP:

Send your business card out with *every* piece of mail, including all bills. Who knows where your card will land, and who might just be looking for someone to type up their manuscript, or play, or .....

Networking means putting your face in front of the people who can use your services, and it also tells other people that you're available. I've always found marketing my business to be one of the most challenging and creative parts of running it. Make an effort every day to spend at least one hour devoted exclusively to finding new customers. Not only will your business continue to grow, new customers mean new and different types of projects which will keep you interested and your enthusiasm high.

Why does networking work so well? For the same reason people buy brand name products. They trust the things they know, or things other people tell them about. If someone has met you at a Chamber of Commerce lunch, or heard about you from a business associate, you are no longer an unknown ..... *you have credibility.*

Cold Calling

I don't know of *anyone* who likes this method of getting new business, but I also don't know anyone (that's successful) who doesn't do it. Cold calling is exactly what the name implies. You get on the telephone, call someone you've never met, and try and convince them that they need your service. It's nerve wracking, anxiety producing, and it works!

One of the best tricks I've learned is to have your "script" already written and in front of you before you pick up the phone—and always make sure you're talking to the right person, the person who will actually be able to say *"Yes! I do have some things I need typed for my presentation next week."*

There are five rules to successful cold calling. Learn them, respect them and most of all, don't get discouraged.

- *Always make sure the prospect has time to talk to you.*
- *Always keep the conversation brief.*
- *Always thank the person for their time.*
- *Always ask if you can send them information.*
- *Always follow up after you've sent the information.*

Here's a sample script for you to follow: "Hello, this is Mary Smith of xxx Typing Service. I offer typing services for businesses like yours—may I send you some information about my services? There's no obligation, and I have an introductory offer, 20% off on your first job. (Confirm address) I'll call you in a week or so to make sure you received the information and to answer any questions you might have. Thank you for your time, and have a good day!"

Public Relations

Public relations is deceptively simple, and is nothing more than getting your name and the name of your business in front of the people you want to become your customers. Even if you've never been required to actively promote yourself, this is a very natural activity. And it can be fun!

Simply stated, public relations is a highly cost-effective way to communicate with your customers. While advertising consists primarily of print space or air time that must be bought, public relations coverage typically comes *free of charge!*

A successful PR campaign can achieve many of the same results as advertising in reaching your target audience with a desired message. It can also increase sales and visibility. Sometimes it's hard to distinguish between advertising and public relations, but just remember: *Advertising is bought* by the advertiser (you), who has complete control of the message. Public Relations depends on another person endorsing your word processing services.

When you use free publicity to secure media coverage, you give up control over the message. By sending a press release or discussing your business with a reporter, the reporter has the final authority over how the subject matter is treated. If you are lucky enough to get someone from your local newspaper to write an article about you and your business, remember it is the reporter's job to ask as many questions as possible to get the information. Try not to become defensive, or take the questions personally.

Just for a moment, think about the many activities you've taken part in: church, school, PTA, volunteering of any kind. All of these groups needed someone to promote what they did, and they also needed other people to help them achieve their goals. Publicity for your word processing business requires the very same things.

In fact, if you've ever served as a volunteer on a committee, baked cookies for Little League or helped run a fund raising rummage sale, chances are you've already done some public relations and promoted your name. Now all that remains is connecting your name to your new business and letting everyone know that you're ready to work.

Most local newspapers are eager for information on new businesses, especially those started and run by women. Begin paying close attention to the business section, names and faces columns, and feature stories written about your business community. Your daily newspaper is just one source for you to get publicity about your business. Think also of local radio and TV stations, the church bulletin, or those free weekly shopper magazines.

When you're ready to accept clients and new business, it's time to write a press release and send it to everyone! Don't just concentrate on your own community. Almost every home-based business person I know tries to work with all businesses within a hundred mile radius. This wasn't possible only a few years ago, but with that trusty Fax machine, your ability to do business from a distance is greatly increased.

Writing a Press Release

Never written a press release before? It's easy. Just remember the old reporter's five rules:

- *Who* – You!
- *What* – Your New Word Processing Business!
- *When* – Did You Open For Business?
- *Why* – Because There Was A Need!
- *Where* – Can They Find You?

A sample Press Release would look like this:

FOR IMMEDIATE RELEASE

Contact: Mary Jones (444) 555-1212

Date: January 1, 1995

MARY JONES OPENS

TYPING SERVICE IN RULE CITY

Mary Jones, formerly of ABC Company, has opened a new typing-word processing service at 123 Center Street, Rule City.

Services include all types of document typing and manuscript preparation including standard business letters, sales reports, speeches, articles, and term papers.

Offering free pick up and delivery, the new service gives special emphasis to medical records processing and transcribing, an area in which Ms. Jones has over 10 years of experience.

###

Positive Press Relations

Knowing the rules for positive press relations will serve you well in all your future business relationships. These rules include:

- Be accurate in everything you say and write
- Always tell the truth
- Never ask to see or approve an article
- Never talk about advertising when discussing an article
- Treat all members of the press equally
- Respect editorial policy and deadlines
- Keep a good attitude if an error occurs

Mail your press release to *every* business editor (including radio and TV) as far away as you want to draw new customers from. Try and address it directly to the business editor—but if you don't know the editor's name, that's OK, it will be passed along.

You can increase the chances of your press release making it into the newspaper by enclosing a photo of yourself. Please, no snapshots of you on your last vacation! If you don't have a businesslike head shot (from the waist up), most print shops can now do passport photography. The charge is minimal, and you can have copies made at your local drugstore.

If you should ever have the opportunity to be a sponsor of any type of community event, do it! Getting your business name attached to fundraising, philanthropic or charitable activities is one of the best ways to build a great name for yourself and your business. It's also a great way to generate more free exposure by using what's called a PSA, or Public Service Announcement.

Most radio and television stations will run PSAs of 10, 20 or even 30 seconds in length free of charge if they are for events that raise money for nonprofit organizations. You should mail your PSA to the station about a month before the event, and they will begin airing it about two weeks before. You can't say much in thirty seconds, so keep the information brief while still including the necessary facts.

A sample Public Service Announcement would look like this:

PUBLIC SERVICE ANNOUNCEMENT - :30 SECONDS

CONTACT: (YOUR NAME)

ADDRESS: (YOUR ADDRESS)

PHONE NUMBER: (YOUR PHONE NUMBER)

:30 SECOND PSA - HALLOWEEN CONTEST

(sample copy)

You can be a winning witch this Halloween by entering the XYZ costume contest. There's lots of prizes and a party for the kids beginning at 6:30 P.M., Saturday, October 31, at 123 Main Street. Don't miss the fun, sponsored by (YOUR BUSINESS NAME) with all proceeds going to FFF Charity.

If you're not sure how you could use PSAs to help your business, sit down with your family, close friends, or business associates and ask them to help you come up with ideas. With a little creative brainstorming, you can probably create a fun and easy promotion that will get you, and your business, out of the closet and into the spotlight in your local community!

Chapter 13: Customer Service

Your word processing business will flourish if you always remember that you will *stay* in business because of your customers. On the other hand, no customers mean no business! One happy customer can turn into ten more. One angry ex-client can do enough damage to send you back to the *nine to five* office routine.

We all know the sad state customer service is in these days, so let's sit down right now and make a list of the most awful things you've ever encountered as a customer: rudeness, indifference, poor workmanship, overpricing—the list could go on forever. The success of your business will depend on how you deal with those very same issues, and because you are the *only* employee, if one of your customers is unhappy, there's only one person responsible. *You.*

We know from experience that the customer is *not* always right, but if you want to stay in business you'll never tell him so. Rude, demanding, arrogant customers don't have to remain *your* customers. You can ever-so-sweetly be too busy to accommodate them and refer them to another typist. Save your good name and eliminate the problem at the same time.

I'd like to share a little piece that I wrote years ago that was published in *Jest Magazine*. It's as true for me today as it was when I wrote it, and I hope it will give you some insight:

The Phone's Ringing .....

I am an entrepreneur ..... and a woman. I routinely pass the magazine quizzes that ask "Should You Start Your Own Business?" I am on intimate terms with the Small Business Administration. Yesterday I was propositioned by my 86 year old mentor from the Retired Executives Association. (I was flattered, and hope that when I'm 86 I'll want to proposition someone!)

My mother-in-law, who for the past thirty-two years has been a mindlessly happy employee of the Federal Government, considers me employably unstable. And still ..... I am an entrepreneur.

Lest you think me a small-time operator, consider this amazing feat. I once made it into the ranks of upper management in a Fortune 500 empire. During this creatively comatose period of my life, I began listening to and almost believing the unsolicited opinions of my potential in the corporate jungle.

> "She's so-o-o bright ... someday she'll learn
> to control that aggressiveness. She'd do great
> selling cars."

Somehow, I did manage to conform but I never truly fit in. Granted, my methods were unconventional, but then sales in my division averaged 39.4% higher than any other. I never understood the nasty rumors emanating from Accounting that I intentionally ignored policy.

You see, my mother taught me (from the breast) that money, profits, and market share talk ..... loudly. To politely surmise a scenario familiar to many entrepreneurs, they won. I left, and on surprisingly good terms, too.

So, once again I find myself unfettered by routine, ready to create yet another challenge. Of my own admission, I feel the same excitement I did when at nineteen I invested my birthday money in women's designer "seconds" (a deal through my Uncle Hymie) and resold them to my mother's friends at slightly above retail. Numerous challenges have manifested over the years, most profitable, some not.

What's really important is the fact that I keep trying, and I still quiver at the thought "I can make it happen!"

Hmmmmm, there's this moderately successful general contractor I know that's looking for a new partner. But wait! The phone's ringing.

It's probably my mother-in-law.

That general contractor and I did become partners, and he taught me more about customer service than I'd learned in twenty years. Rick was the friendly face behind the counter of that *friendly skies* airline until he got laid off and decided that he too wanted to work for himself. This wiry little Italian from New York loved building things, and became a one-man construction company. Need new front doors designed, built and installed? *"No problem. I can do that!"* From reroofing an entire house, to replacing a back door screen, his answer was always the same. *"No, problem. I can do that!"*

So how did I, a writer, become a part of Rick's business? Well, he needed to be out in the field doing the actual renovation work, and he also needed someone to answer the phone, take care of the books, and promote the business. It was a perfect match. Talking to prospective customers every day was what I was good at, and at the end of each workday, we'd sit down and I would tell Rick what work requests came in. His reply was always the same. "No *problem. I can do that!"*

This is an area you will also probably want to explore, finding ways to make your typing service fit into the needs of other businesses. Maybe it will mean developing relationships with various office managers who can call you to fill in (working either at home or even at their office) when someone on staff calls in sick, or goes on vacation. You could act as your own "temp" service.

This has become a very lucrative part of my own home-based business. I recently got a call from a large nonprofit theater group whose public relations manager was going on maternity leave. They really didn't have a large enough staff for someone else to take over her duties, so they asked me if I would manage their public relations department for ninety days. It's turned out to be a perfect arrangement for both of us. I love the opportunity to get out of my "office" for a few hours each day, and they know that the many functions of keeping their activities visible are being taken care of. Think of ways that you too can "fill in" for businesses and companies that could use your service.

As the first (and only) person your customers will come into contact with, your business will surely thrive if you adopt Rick-the-handyman's can-do attitude. I'm not suggesting that you tackle jobs that you're not quite

ready to take on, or that may be too big for you to handle, or that you can't meet the customer's deadline.

However, before you turn down work that might cause you a little stress because you've never done it before, take a few extra moments with your customer to ask the right questions and then offer to call them back with an answer. One of the greatest things about working for yourself is the many different kinds of projects that you can become involved in.

Always try to take a *"No problem ... I can do that!"* attitude and you'll never be bored with your business. You'll continue to grow as a professional, and your customers will quickly learn that they can count on you to offer solutions to their problems.

I'd like to take this opportunity to publicly thank my friend and former partner Rick for everything he taught me about customer service, human nature, and the joy of working for myself. Although he never wanted to "grow" his business any larger and I was ready to go off on my own, his customers are the most loyal I've ever seen.

Since the majority of your business will begin on the phone, it's vital to develop your telephone presentation long before the first customer calls. The most important thing you can do to establish immediate rapport is to *make your customers feel welcome!*

Enthusiasm is contagious, and your cheerful, upbeat voice on the phone will immediately make your caller eager to tell you what he needs. A flat, monotone greeting that sounds like you really aren't interested in your caller will only make it more difficult to gain the confidence of someone who has no idea what you or your business is about. Enthusiasm breeds confidence.

Mirror, Mirror On The Wall .....

Before Sandra Partenser started her desktop publishing business she did telemarketing sales and customer service for a large software publishing company. I met Sandra through another graphic designer at a Leads networking luncheon, and we immediately hit it off. Over the course of a year, we did a little business together and met for coffee as often as our schedules would allow.

Having earned her living as a professional phone person, Sandra had the most hilarious stories to tell. She told me one thing however that I've shared with everyone I know who deals with the public, on the telephone. She told me to mount a fairly large mirror on the wall, directly in front of where I'd be forced to look at myself whenever I talked on the phone.

Oh! The first few times I answered the phone were awful until I realized that if I smiled at myself in the mirror, it was immediately reflected in my voice. When I smiled, I actually sounded happier and more cheerful. If I had a difficult customer, I often stuck my tongue out and made faces at myself, even though the grouch on the other end of the phone couldn't see it, and I usually ended up trying not to laugh out loud! When you get a really *great* phone call, the smile is genuine and can energize you for the entire day. Research has shown that deliberately thinking pleasant thoughts, and changing your facial expression from frown to smile really does change the way your brain reacts. This conscious effort to improve your demeanor allows the release of endorphins which clears your thinking and creates an aura of hope. The mirror trick is one of those tips that sounds terribly corny, but try it anyway. The rewards are enormous.

But let's talk for just a moment about those crabby, unreasonable people who try to make your life miserable. *The customer you can never satisfy!* Don't be too quick to skip over this section, believing that you'll never have one. We all do, no matter how hard we try to do everything right. The truly awful customer is usually miserable to begin with, and nothing you can say or do is going to appease him or her.

Your best defense is to develop early on the skills that will help you recognize those people whom you will never be able to please. Some of the early warning signals may include:

- **Arrogance and condescending attitude**
- **Rudeness and disregard for your policies**
- **Always in a rush**
- **Never offers a 'please' or 'thank you'**
- **Argues over fees**
- **Is never satisfied with the final product**

Remember, *you are the boss.* You own this company. There is absolutely no need to put up with this type of customer. Of course, you will always do your best to meet the needs of your customers, but never allow anyone to intimidate or abuse you in any way.

Beware of customers that try and draw you into an argument or provoke you into losing your temper. Remain calm at all times, and if you find yourself losing control of the situation, simply say "I'm sorry Mr. Jones, I've got another call (or someone's at the door). May I call you right back?" And then hang up. Once you've had time to cool off and decide how *you* want this situation resolved, you can call back and finish the conversation.

Once you've made the decision to purge your client list of a particular problem customer, remove the name from your card file or data base, and the next time he/she calls, make sure you're too busy to accommodate him or her.

The vast majority of my customers are extremely pleasant and enjoyable to work with, but once in awhile I run into a grouch. When I do, I always remember what the famous psychoanalyst Clara Thompson said, *"If you want unconditional enthusiasm and love, get a dog."* I have two.

Ethics

There may come a time when you are faced with a request from a customer that you find unethical, illegal or immoral. All business people are faced with these issues. Before you find yourself in a precarious situation, give some thought as to how you want to run your business.

As employees, most of the decisions relating to how a business will be conducted are predetermined by management. As the sole owner of your word processing service, you will be responsible for the type of work you accept and the clients you engage. If you imagine that **your** name is at the top of every letterhead, projects that could be ethically questionable will jump out at you with a red flag.

Are you responsible for the contents of the documents that you prepare? There's no easy way to answer this question, but if you even slightly suspect any type of misrepresentation of information, take the safest route and decline the work.

For example, let's say a local real estate person asks you to type up a letter to someone who lives in another state, and you know that the parcel of land he's describing has been condemned because of toxic problems. If the unsuspecting customer buys the land and later sues your client for misrepresentation, would you also be considered liable because you prepared the letter? I don't know, but I wouldn't take the chance and neither should you. Why risk your good name and business! Use your best judgment and common sense when accepting work from one-time, unknown clients and run as fast as you can from anything that doesn't feel right.

The second issue of ethical responsibility is confidentiality. This is especially critical if you plan on specializing in legal or medical documentation. If you've worked in these fields prior to starting your typing service, you already know the professional code of conduct. If you are new to this type of word processing, just remember that whatever information you may learn while preparing documents must *never* leave your office.

My friend Sarah was a legal secretary for twenty-five years. She retired last year and says she never wants to type another legal brief as long as she lives, but she has begun writing her first novel! A who-done-it, of course! She calls me from time to time for inspiration and help, so I asked her about the confidentiality thing. Her very words were, *"Honey, I didn't even talk to my husband about the cases in the office."* She confirmed the need for absolute silence concerning conversations between attorneys and their clients. She also offered this, *"If you don't remember nothin', 'ya can't tell 'em nothin'!"* Good advice from an old pro. I can't wait to read her book.

Say What You Mean & Mean What You Say!

In business, you're only as good as your word. Don't make promises you can't keep; don't pretend you're something you're not; and no matter what, tell your customers the truth.

Nothing will ruin your business quicker than a bad reputation. Whether it's because you missed an important deadline, botched a crucial paragraph or double billed someone in error, your *attention to detail* is what will make or break your word processing business.

Honesty and integrity mean that you will stand by your word, you will do exactly what you have agreed to do, and do it to the very best of your ability. Decide right now that no matter what else you do, *you will guarantee customer satisfaction and give them more than they expect, every time.* If you're not committed to doing the very best work you can do for your customers, you won't have any!

Don't worry about making some mistakes. Everyone in business does. When you find yourself in trouble, immediately call your customer and tell them the truth. Also tell them what you're going to do to fix the problem and how long it will take.

"I'm sorry, but ....." has saved me from professional ruin more times than I care to admit. Say that sentence ten times, right now. Then when you have to call a customer it won't sound like some foreign phrase that you've never heard before!

When I was new at this game and thought I could do anything and knew everything, as a favor to a friend I agreed to edit a book I had no business even touching. It was so far over my head, I didn't even know where to begin. As I've said before, I'm not a technophile, and I don't especially know how things work, only that they're supposed to. Anyway, this manuscript was so technical that every time I picked it up and read more than three pages, I began to itch. So I quit reading and the manuscript eventually found its way to the bottom of a drawer. But the itching continued because I hadn't really dealt with the cause. I was too embarrassed to tell my friend or the author that I couldn't do it.

I guess you'd like to know how I got out of this one ..... well, I moved away. I'm not proud of this, and I did eventually call my friend to tell him I had returned the manuscript. I'm not proud of the way I handled this situation, but I learned a lot about myself and what it means to *do what you say you're going to do*. No excuses. If you don't feel qualified to take on a particular project, be honest with yourself and your customer. You'll gain a great deal of self-respect and save yourself many sleepless nights. And know also that with more experience, there will come a time when you *can* do anything you say you can.

This is also a good time to look at the need for keeping your sense of humor about your business. Sometimes things just don't go right. It's not your fault, and expecting things to always be predictable, neat and permanent will only add to your frustration. This is when we must try harder to remember that life (and work) need to be kept in perspective.

If in the process of mangled situations you can recognize and accept the foibles in yourself and your customers, things become so much simpler. Never withhold a good chuckle from yourself or your customers! Modern medicine has finally admitted that laughter is genuinely good for you. A good belly-laugh calms the nervous system, improves immune functions and actually massages internal organs. All this for free!

Deadlines

As the proud owner of a new typing business, you probably won't have an overwhelming amount of work to do in the early days. Deadline pressure may seem like something *other* people have to deal with, but just wait! It can all change with one simple phone call.

"Hello, is this Mary Jones Typing Service?"

"Yes, it is. This is Mary Jones, how may I help you?"

"Oh, Mary! I'm so glad I caught you. I need your help! My boss just called and said the report that I've been working on for two months that was supposed to be ready next Tuesday must be on his desk by five tomorrow afternoon! Can you type it for me?"

Mary Jones, being new in business says .....

"Well, yes, of course I can."

Welcome to the world of deadline mania. Can Mary get this report done in 24 hours? Well, yes if she works every one of them. She will also hopefully build in a hefty rush charge, which her customer will gladly pay. If Mary actually does what she said she would do, she will also have made a customer for life who will tell *everyone* she knows how Mary Jones saved the day.

Deadlines are a crucial part of your typing service, and can actually work in your favor if you know how to maintain control of your working environment. I'm one of those people who thrives on deadline pressure, especially if there is a monetary incentive. I love performance bonuses!

In the beginning however, it's best to not squeeze yourself too tight, especially if you have heavy family responsibilities. Kids don't understand deadlines and really don't care. All they want to know is why you can't drive them to soccer practice and do we get to order pizza again tonight?

Allow yourself plenty of time to complete each job you accept, and be sure to find out if the customer has any flexibility regarding the absolute deadline for completion. If you run into problems and know you're not going to have the work ready when the customer expects it, call them as soon as you know that. Never call a customer an hour before the project is due and say, *"I'm sorry, but ....."*

Building Your Portfolio

As your business begins to grow and your list of satisfied clients expands, it's time to put together a portfolio of your work. Don't let the big word scare you, as we tend to think only artists or designers would use this type of marketing tool. A portfolio is nothing more than a presentation of the work you've done that you will show prospective clients, and it can be as simple as a three-ring binder.

If you're still working at your job, now may be the perfect time to look back over projects you've completed and make copies of those that were particularly difficult, or those that you were very proud of. This could be the beginning of your portfolio. If you're just starting out, don't worry because you don't have anything to show new clients. You soon will!

What can a portfolio do for you? Let's say you've sent a direct mail cover letter to someone your sister told you needed extra typing help during tax season. You've also included a copy of the article that appeared in your local newspaper about your new word processing service and a business card. Three days later the phone rings and it's the owner of XYZ Tax Service who would like to meet with you to discuss how you might work with them. Your portfolio is the tangible, visual evidence that you really can do what you say. That you've done it before ..... and that you are a professional with proven experience. Chances are you'll get the work!

What should your portfolio include? As I said before, samples of various kinds of your work, preferably on (client) company letterhead, plus any letters of recommendation that you get from satisfied customers.

Ask for Recommendations

Always ask for a letter of recommendation when you have a customer who's really happy with your work. Whether it's because you completed a rush job before a deadline, or because you have developed a long-standing relationship, get in the habit of asking every customer for a letter of reference or recommendation.

Make copies of these letters and use them as another piece of your marketing pie. Send a copy of the letter along with your cover letter to prospective customers. The recommendation of a satisfied client is the best marketing tool you can have.

Your Resume

A copy of your most recent resume should be the first page in your portfolio. You can list your most recent employment and every other job you've had that will lend credibility to your new venture. If you have educational experience and specific technical skills, certificates or a degree, those should also be listed. Take some time to write your resume carefully, because even though you're not going to use it to apply for a job working for someone else, you will be using it to get work. There are many excellent books available at the library which will show you how to format and type your "Self-Employment" resume.

Your portfolio can also include a *Client List*. This is a printed page that I put on my own letterhead that lists clients who when contacted will give me an excellent verbal recommendation. I use my client list as a way for prospective customers to see and contact other clients I have done business with. I only give this *confidential* Client List to those customers I know will be discreet, and who I believe are ready to give me work. When putting together your own Client List, be sure to ask your customers for permission to be included, as some do not want their names or company listed for reasons of confidentiality.

Once a month spend some time updating your portfolio, removing older samples and inserting new ones. There are several good reasons for taking the time to do this, but the most important one is to visually remind yourself that your business continues to grow and that you *are* successful!

Knowing that there will be times when you have little work, and times when you feel totally overwhelmed, spending an hour with your portfolio reinforces your commitment to your business and confirms your tangible success. One person I shared this tip with goes a step further and writes on the back of each sample how much money the job made her. On those days when your phone doesn't ring, just pick up your portfolio and remember that it will again.

Rejection—Don't Take It Personally!

Being rejected by prospective customers is a natural part of being in business for yourself. Accept it, try to remember that they're not rejecting you as a person, and that no matter what, *you can't take it personally!*

There are so many reasons why you may not get a particular job that

it would be impossible to list them all. Being a one-woman-band sometimes makes you particularly vulnerable to feeling personally rejected, but it's important that you let your skin thicken a bit. If you are aggressively promoting your business to prospective customers, you automatically increase the probability of rejection. But the numbers don't lie, and even if you're told "no" by the ten people you call, the next one may become your very best client!

Jim Stosley left the retail automobile business because he wanted to spend more time with his sons, ages eight and five. He had grown weary of working every weekend, and never seeing his boys before they went to bed. He wanted more control over his working hours, and after watching the independent detailers who came on the car lot every day, decided he could do that too.

Jim already had many contacts in the auto industry, but seemed to get very little of the business he went after in the first six months. (Wisely, he had planned his transition to self-employment well by saving a lot of money, and his wife was securely employed and also very supportive). Having been a car salesman for many years, Jim was used to customer rejection, but couldn't figure out why the dealerships weren't sending him any business. He'd been very aggressive with his marketing materials and flyers, and spend at least half of each day cold-calling the service managers on the car lots, trying to get their business.

Finally, in frustration Jim asked a potential customer point-blank, *"Why aren't you using my service? What am I doing wrong?"* He was amazed to learn that his prices were *too low*, and the dealership was skeptical that he could really do the job. That problem was easily solved, Jim immediately raised his prices to match his competition and has now been in business very successfully for six years.

The lesson here is: If you've tried everything you know to get your foot in the door of a business you want to work with and can't, *ask them why!* You may never get their business, but you won't spend any more time wondering why they have rejected you. You'll know, and can move on to your next prospect. There may also be a very simple reason (as in Jim's case) that you can correct. You'll never know if you don't ask.

Dealing With Isolation

As much as you will grow to love the freedom and challenge of your home-based typing business, one downside of self-employment is spending the majority of your working hours by yourself.

If like me, you've grown weary of office politics and the feeling that you spent entire days just trying to get something *(anything)* done at work, then the solitude of your own personal work space will feel like a gift from the gods. And it is. Almost every home-based worker I know, when asked what they love most about working at home, will immediately talk about the peace and quiet.

The down side of all this peace and quiet is that sometimes you actually miss the water-cooler gossip. Socialization in the workplace is one of those unwritten benefits, and while I don't miss the constant interruptions of office life, sometimes I do miss being around people. I'm the kind of person that gets energized from other people, and there are certain days when the thought of sitting by myself, alone again, makes me question my solitary career choice. But not for long!

If you realize early on that there *will* be times when you feel lonely and cut off from the mainstream work force, you'll also know how to deal with it. I called several people and posed this very question, asking how they turned those negative feelings into positive. Here are the top three suggestions:

Get Out of the House

Take a shower, get really dressed up and go downtown and have lunch with another home-worker, or former business associate. This is not just a social lunch, but a working lunch where you will talk about professional issues, problems, customers, etc.

Take the Day Off

Unless you have a pressing deadline, this would be the perfect day to go to an afternoon movie. Or go shopping, or visit your mother, or have your hair done. It almost feels like you're a kid ditching school, to be out *playing* in the middle of the week when the rest of the working world has no choice in the matter. The really great part is no crowds.

Clean Your Office

You'll still feel like you're working, but it's a different kind of productivity. Rearrange the furniture, throw something out or hang a new poster. When you open the door the next morning, you'll be energized by what you've accomplished, and ready to get to work again.

Do Someone A Favor

You can really get creative with this one. Is there a relative or friend you haven't called in a while? Is there a next-door neighbor who would appreciate flowers from your garden? Could you make something special for dinner tonight? You get the idea. There's no better way to feel ten feet tall than to do someone else a favor—and as a home-based worker, you have the flexibility to make it happen!

Do Unto Others

To maintain good relationships with your clients, it's a good idea to keep the Golden Rule in mind. Sure, it's nice when a client sends flowers or a special thank you note—but have you ever thought of doing something similar in return for them?

There are some occasions when gifts and notes to your clients are in order. The Christmas and Hanukkah holidays are an obvious choice. But remember, it's not so much the particular holiday as the thought that counts. Find an excuse to express your appreciation to your best clients at least once a year.

It's not necessary to spend a lot of money. Even a simple card with a personal, handwritten message will do. As you get to know your clients better over the years, you will naturally learn something about their personal likes and dislikes. When someone mentions that they just love chocolate, you might want to note it on the back of their business card. If you surprise them with a miniature box of chocolates and a special note, it will really make their day!

Another good thing to do is to call your clients on a regular basis—once every few months or so—just to say hello and check up on what their needs are. While it's possible to make a pest of yourself if you call too often, one call every two or three months to your active clients is likely to be appreciated and to make you appear especially interested in customer service. You'll find even more tips along this line in the next chapter.

You get the idea. Make sure you reap good things by sowing the seeds of thankfulness and appreciation today! You'll stand out in the crowd, and your clients will remember you with fondness—not only today, but also when it comes time for the next big job!

Chapter 14:
Finding and Keeping
Customers

We briefly touched on developing your client list in Chapter 12, Advertising, Marketing and Public Relations. Now let's take a closer look at the next phase of bringing in those customers that will get your business off and running.

You've probably been making a prospective customer list in your head ever since you started reading this book. That's great, because feeding your hungry baby (your business) is something that will become an important part of your life. Customers come and go for a variety of reasons, and just as you wouldn't want to drive the same car for your entire life, neither would you want to work with the same clients forever.

Again, one of the many benefits of your word processing business is your ability to grow as a professional and to learn new skills. The quickest way for this to happen is to have a customer ask you to do something that you've never done before. It's a little scary saying *"Yes, I can do that!"* when you've never done it, but also know in your heart that you will do whatever it takes to make it happen.

It's possible that you may want to develop your typing service by specializing in just one area, one that you already have a good deal of experience in. In that case, you will also know where to find those particular customers, and probably also know best how to solicit their business. For example, if you used to be a legal secretary, you will already know a large number of lawyers; and if you're currently tied into a professional network of any kind, signing up your initial clients will be a relatively simple matter.

To continue this example of a business seeking legal typing work: once your business cards have been printed and you've created either a flyer or cover letter, a direct mail campaign aimed at members of your state and/or local Bar Association should get you an immediate response. Additional mailings can be done using the Yellow Pages for the name and address of attorneys in your community.

Narrowing your marketing focus to one specific industry simplifies the search for customers, but it may also eliminate many other companies that could use your services. If you are planning to focus on just one type of business client, it would still be wise to keep your options open for future business opportunities.

If you've decided to be what I call a generalist, meaning an all-purpose typing service, then your quest for customers takes on a different meaning. Your options are limitless, and so are the ways in which you can solicit new customers.

Let's go back to the basics for a moment and look again at the quickest ways of finding customers.

- **Family & Friends**
- **Former Employers & Contacts**
- **Fictitious Business Name Filings**
- **County Business License Applications**
- **Educational Institutions**
- **Networking**
- **Newspaper Business & Service Directory**
- **Church & Club Affiliations**
- **Businesses You Patronize**
- **Chamber Of Commerce**
- **Yellow Pages**

I keep a file folder labeled "Prospects," and every time I hear about a new business, or someone getting promoted, or *any* related business information I stick it in that folder. I regularly read the local business section of all area newspapers, subscribe to a three county monthly business magazine, and find the Chamber of Commerce monthly newsletters invaluable for culling new prospects.

This is one part of your marketing plan that needs almost daily attention. Once every week, I sit down and go through my "Prospects" folder and either send a letter with my business card or call the person directly.

This is what is known in sales as the *pipeline* theory. As your business evolves, it becomes necessary to have new business prospects percolating in all areas of your pipeline. Here's an example:

> *Just as the XYZ Medical Group (one of your best customers) decides to relocate to another state, you learn that ABC Attorneys are expanding their practice and are in dire need of additional word processing help. You heard about the ABC expansion plan from your brother's father-in-law (a lawyer) and immediately contacted them with information about your business. That was nearly a year ago, long before you found out you'd be losing the XYZ Medical account. Now ABC Attorneys becomes one of your best customers!*

Customers come and go, some bringing short-term projects, others you could do business with for years—but a customer for life is about as probable in today's workplace as a job for life. The important thing to remember is that to keep your business and bank account healthy, new business development is an activity that you need to pay attention to every day.

An absolute must for your home-office bookshelf is the incredible *Guerrilla Marketing* by Jay Levinson. Buy this book and reread it every few months until you understand this simple concepts required to keep customers flowing to you. To jump start your sales and marketing efforts, you may also want to subscribe to his *Guerrilla Marketing Newsletter* (800-748-6444) which I've found keeps me in touch with the newest ideas for promoting my own business.

I asked Saul Preston, a retired advertising executive to give me his five most important tips for getting and keeping customers. He laughed and said, *"Only five .....?"* Here they are:

• **Be sure you talk to the person who can use you:** *Don't waste your time trying to sell your services to the wrong person. Go to the top.*

• **Build your client's trust:** *Clients are afraid to buy anything from an unknown. Build trust at any cost.*

• **Always ask your clients for a referral:** *Using a mutual client's name is the quickest way to get in a new door.*

• **Make sure you know what your customer needs:** *Never let a customer leave if you have any questions about what he expects from you.*

• **Remember to ask for the sale:** *You won't get the business if you don't ask for it.*

How To Keep 'Em Coming Back For More

Repeat customers and referrals are the lifeblood of any business, no matter how large or small. It takes a lot of time and energy to solicit and develop a new client relationship. Established customers are like money in the bank, and should be treated the same way ... *do everything within your power to keep them there!*

The most important thing you can do is keep in touch with your best customers. I'm not suggesting that you call them every week, bugging them for business. But drop them a personal note occasionally, or clip an article you know would be of interest and send it off. If you receive any awards, are the guest speaker at a seminar, or head up a committee and it appears in the newspaper, make copies and send them to your customers.

Keeping your business visible is one of the surest ways to get repeat business. I can't remember how many times I've called someone just to say hello and their first comment is "I'm *so glad you called, I was just thinking of you!*" It doesn't always culminate in a paying project or job, but it seems that the more visible I make myself, the busier I am. It's important that no matter how large or small your customer list is, that you create an efficient system for keeping track of customer names, addresses and phone numbers. Every person you *ever* contact about business should be added to your card file.

There are many ways to manage customer information, and if you're working on a computer, most word processing programs have the ability to do this for you. *(Of course, you still have to be the one to enter the information. Computers are wonderful but they don't run themselves!)*

I've found that even though I do use my computer to track customer activity, I've never been able to give up my trusty old card file. There's something soothing about being able to write on a customers index card instead of just typing information. I use my Rolodex for all sorts of things, including recording the date every time I talk to someone, and if it's important, what the conversation was about. I know a lot of people who keep this type of information in their computer files, and that works too, but I still like the old fashioned feel of flipping through my Rolodex.

Use your card file to identify people who have become clients, their birthdays, kids' names, hobbies, professional affiliations and any newsworthy items you may come across. Whenever I see something about one of my clients (or even someone I'd like to have as a client) in the newspaper, I clip it out and send it with a note and business card.

Last year a local software company advertised in the newspaper classified section for someone to write and edit a user manual. I immediately sent them my standard marketing letter, samples of my writing, and a copy of an article I'd written for a computer magazine. After two weeks and no response, I called the department manager in charge of the project and asked if he'd received my information. He was less than cordial, saying my experience did not match what they were looking for. I tried to get more information from him, but it was obvious he didn't want to talk to me so I graciously thanked him for his time, asked him to keep me in mind for future writing assignments, and hung up.

The mirror above my telephone reflected my agitation, and the stinging rejection. But I was on deadline for a magazine review I was writing and quickly got back to work, erasing the incident from my mind. Temporarily, anyway. Several months passed and as I was reading the business news one morning, there was the same project manager's picture above the story of his appointment as President of a *competing* software company.

I immediately sat down and wrote him a letter of congratulations and also included my standard request to be considered for any future assignments. Two days later his new secretary called to schedule a lunch meeting between me and her boss. To cut to the chase, this man has become one of my greatest supporters and his company is currently my #1 client! Keep your face and name in front of every current customer and every potential customer, *every chance you get.*

Stay in Circulation

In your business, the day will come when you reach a certain comfort level. You will have several large clients and a pool of smaller clients that keep a steady stream of work flowing in your direction.

At that point in time, it's easy to start taking work for granted. Believe me, I know, because it happened to me. I'll never forget the year I lost my three biggest clients, all at once! One went bankrupt, one moved out of the area, and the other was on the verge of bankruptcy.

Now, I could have survived those calamities if I had kept my pipeline open, as described earlier in this chapter. But had I done that? No. I had been so busy working for those three big clients that I hadn't taken the time to develop any new contacts. My pipeline was dry, and I had to start from scratch.

What did I do? Everything we've talked about in this chapter. I attended every networking meeting I could find. I printed up new business cards, letterhead, and envelopes and did a mailing to local businesses. I passed out my new cards wherever I went. I called all my old clients looking for referrals. I made cold calls to an incredible number of people, and that's something I just hate to do. But I was scared, so I was motivated.

I'm happy to say that all my hard work paid off. Within two months I had saved my business. I picked up two significant new clients almost right away. One responded to a letter I did as part of my mailing, and the other was the result of a cold call. Within the next six months, I had a whole new client roster going. What a relief—and what a scare!

Don't wait to learn the hard way, like I did, about the value of networking and keeping up with your clients on an everyday basis. Nothing is written in stone. The clients who form the bulk of your income today could very well be gone tomorrow, usually for reasons that have nothing to do with you personally.

That's right—no matter how good a job you do, clients will still come and go. So it's up to you to keep your pipeline open. Whether you're just beginning your business, or whether you think you've got it made, networking is the key to finding and keeping customers. So just do it!

Chapter 15: Making Money and Getting Paid

The most tangible form of success in your word processing business is your bank account. That's not to say that the other reasons that prompted you to become an independent entrepreneur aren't just as valuable—it's just that when we can look at our checkbooks and visibly see the results of our hard work, we have proof positive that we're successful!

Getting paid for the work you do validates your professionalism. Money not only pays the bills, for the small business person it also symbolizes your ability to triumph over those who said you were crazy to try! Make no mistake .... *the money you earn is important*. But also just as important are the other things your business provides, such as more time with your family, more creativity in your work life, and more flexibility to choose how much and when you will work.

Your attitude about being paid for the work that you do, and the degree of professionalism that you bring to this part of your business will be directly reflected in how your customers perceive you and your services. This is a very important issue and one that you'll need to become comfortable with the first time the phone rings and you answer *"No problem! I can do that."*

Always keep in mind that you didn't go into business for yourself to go broke. Often due to a lack of experience, or modesty, many newly self-employed people undervalue their time and services. This is easily correctable, and before you start accepting customers you should (anonymously) contact your competition to find out the going rate for word processing/typing services in your area.

There's nothing underhanded about this. Large companies use this technique all the time to find out if their products, services and pricing are in line with other manufacturers. And, they never call up and say, *"Hey! I make widgets just like you. How much do yours cost?"*

It's easy in the beginning to be quick to accept any and all work that comes your way. In time, however, you'll find that your business will survive *and* prosper with a smaller amount of work that's priced realistically. If you sell yourself and your services too cheaply (remember Jim Stosley and his auto detailing business), you'd be better off to just take that time and go see a movie or clean out a closet!

Try to keep an eye on exactly what your home business is costing you. A good rule of thumb is if you value your time at a fixed hourly rate (say $20), and through your business you are still not able to cover your share of the household expenses such as utility bills and mortgage, you're probably not charging enough. Remember too, that many services such as word processing actually gain credibility and prestige if they're priced a little bit higher.

Once your typing service is up and running, if you find yourself working at maximum capacity, accepting every job that walks through your door, and you're still not showing a profit, it may be time to consider raising your rates. Pricing is quite often not a true indicator of the value of your service. Do your homework, find out what the highest price is that you remain competitive with, *and then charge it ..... always with a smile!*

Without a weekly paycheck to deposit, it can sometimes seem like your business isn't really making any money. A trick I learned years ago, and have passed on to everyone I know is from the book *The Richest Man In Babylon* by George S. Clason. The story is told in parable, and the basic is premise is that in order to become truly wealthy, here's what you must do:

HOT TIP:

Ten percent (10%) of *every* dime that passes through your hands goes into a savings account and is never withdrawn. *For Any Reason Or Purpose!*

This way you pay yourself first, before any bills, before the kids allowances, and before the tax man comes. Just knowing that I have money in the bank *(and that no matter what happens, I don't touch it!)* has given me peace of mind and allowed me to remain optimistic about working for myself through the lean times.

Policies & Terms

It's time to take out that trusty notebook again and begin a new chapter: *How I Want To Run My Business*. This exercise is not intended for anyone else's eyes but yours, and it's going to help you define your rules of operation. This doesn't need to be pretty or in any specific form. It's almost like a journal in which you test ideas and theories that will make your business a reflection of your professional values.

When dealing with your customers, to appear confident and professional, you need to have your basic rules of operation firmly in mind. Otherwise, you risk looking indecisive. Confidence breeds confidence. It's disconcerting for a customer to think that the person who is supposed to be an expert (you) and help them, is unsure of how things operate. This is not to say that you'll have an answer to every question you're asked, or that you will immediately know how to handle every project presented to you. It's just that if you want to be perceived as a competent professional, the systems and rules of your word-processing business need to be on the tip of your tongue.

Below I've described some basic concepts that I've found very useful and that help keep me confident. Try them, they may also work for you!

Phone Inquiries and Price Quotes

Because your initial customer contact will probably be on the phone, be very careful not to commit to any job or price until you've actually seen the work to be performed.

It's perfectly o.k. to give your customer a range of pricing, and say *"Well, Mr. Jones, a standard, one page resume can be anywhere from $50 to $100, depending on whether you need me to write and edit it, or if it just needs to be formatted and typed. I really need to take a look at what you have before I give you a definite price."* Never let a customer bully you into giving them a price quote over the phone, for your protection as well as theirs.

A sample customer phone inquiry form that I've found most useful looks like this:

Customer Inquiry Form

Date _____ Time _____

Customer Name _____

Address _____

Phone Number (W) _____ (H) _____

Type Of Job _____

When Needed _____

Pick-Up Or Delivered _____

Number Of Copies _____

Estimate _____

Deposit Received _____

Customer Signature _____

Once you and your client have agreed on price and the specific terms of the work, the customer's signature makes it a binding contract. If there is ever a dispute regarding the nature of your work, this document will prove both your intent and mutual agreement. The Internal Revenue Service also likes to see signed work orders as proof of income for tax purposes. Should your word processing business ever be audited, you'll have tangible proof of exactly what you have done.

The Customer Inquiry Form should also be kept on a clipboard, next to your office telephone. Even if you are unable to accommodate the caller for this particular job, you now know that he is someone who needs and uses your type of service. By getting his name, address and telephone number you can add this prospect to your mailing list and possibly get business from him in the future.

Deposit Agreements

Upon accepting any assignment, always ask for a cash deposit, even if it's your Great Aunt Mary's hairdresser ... or even your Great Aunt Mary! Too many small businesses have too many problems collecting money owed to them because they fail to follow accepted business practices.

If you hire an architect to design your new house, you can bet he won't wait until the blueprints are completed before asking for some sort of payment. Neither should *you* carry the entire burden of doing the work, and then hope and wait to get paid. By asking for one half (50%) of your entire fee up front, you have in essence committed your customer to the job.

One of the worst experiences I ever had was when a *friend* asked me to write, edit, and make one hundred copies of his resume. *"No problem! I can do that!"* And I did. Because he *was* a friend, I felt uncomfortable asking him for my usual up-front deposit. Days passed, and even with repeated phone calls, he never came to pick up his resume.

I finally caught up with him at 6:30 one morning, only to be told that he'd already found a new job and didn't need the resume. No offer to pay me, not even a thank you. Not only was I out the time, but I'd spent *my* hard cash having his resume printed on colored, letter quality stock. At least had I'd gotten a deposit, I could have recovered my costs.

In the beginning, you will probably accept many jobs from family and friends. Just remember to not let personal relationships get in the way of running your business professionally.

Cash, Check or Credit?

As a small, independent business you will probably want to work on a cash-only basis. Unless you start off with large corporate clients, smaller jobs should be paid for at the time you deliver the finished product, preferably in cash or by check. For one time only customers, cash is probably the safest way to ensure payment. If it turns into a repeat customer, then payment by check should be fine.

Do you want to extend credit to your customers? In the beginning, probably not. Credit accounts mean you will have to develop and maintain some sort of accounting system for money owed you. Most small businesses cannot afford the luxury of waiting thirty or sixty days for payment. If you do have corporate type customers, it is perfectly acceptable to present an invoice upon completion of the job, payable upon receipt. This still may not guarantee prompt payment, as the invoice will probably be sent to the accounting department to be paid just like all other invoices. If your client only pays once a month, it could be weeks before you see your money.

As a general rule, it's best for a small business never to let a customer owe them more than they can collect in Small Claims Court. In California that amount is $5,000. Check state regulations for guidelines, but hopefully you'll never have to collect money this way. Always try to keep your customers paid up to date, and if there seems to be a problem, sit down and discuss it with them. If a good customer has an overdue balance with you, it may not be wise to accept more work from them until the previous work has been paid for.

Although you may eventually decide to accept credit cards from your customers, in the beginning it could be more aggravation than it's worth. It

can be difficult to find a bank that will grant a new, small business Merchant status, and you will also have to include the bank's flat monthly fees plus a percentage of each transaction into your pricing to cover those costs. If you're set on offering your customers credit card payment privileges, a visit to your local bank is definitely in order.

If you have new customers that insist on being billed, what you may want to do is accept the job along with a Master Card or Visa number, and the agreement that if the customer does not pay as agreed within thirty days, you will charge the amount to their credit card.

Customer Satisfaction

Although the subject of how to deal effectively with clients can never be fully covered, the Golden Rule applies as well in business as in any other situation. Maybe more. Always treat your customers with respect and remember without them you have no business, no paycheck, no nothing!

Knowing how little effort seems to be placed on customer satisfaction these days, here is your opportunity to actually do something, to stand apart from the rest and change all of that. As the owner of your own business, you *can* make a difference in how people are treated. That's one of those intangible (and wonderful!) benefits of self-employment.

Giving that little extra effort, taking time to *really listen* to your customers and make them feel that you truly care about them will guarantee your success. You'll probably make some new friends along the way, too.

Customer Comment Cards

One of the most valuable tools you can utilize is the customer comment card. If you want to really find out how your service and product measures up, ask your customers! Give them an open forum to tell you how you're doing. You'll learn what works and what doesn't, and if you ask, they'll probably tell you how to fix it. You can design your own customer comment form using any style that works for you. It can be a letter, postcard, or even a phone call to find out if your customer is happy with the job you did.

Just be sure to ask the right questions. People tend not to be as honest on the phone if they're unhappy, but will usually give you plenty of information on a form that they can fill out and return to you anonymously.

Part of my weekly office administration is sending out comment cards, and it's the one thing I never fail to do. I learned this trick from a friend who works as a customer service manager for a large hotel chain. He told me that an unhappy customer will usually not bother to tell you why he's dissatisfied, he just won't use you ever again.

If however, you give him the opportunity to share his frustrations and try to fix the situation, chances are he'll give you another try. So as soon as I complete a job for a customer, I add his name to my folder titled "Follow-Up," and then send him a postage-paid post card which asks the following questions:

In Order That I May Best Serve Your Needs,

Please Answer The Following Questions:

• **Did You Get What You Asked For?**   _____

• **Did You Pay A Fair Price?**   _____

• **Would You Use My Services Again?**   _____

• **On A Scale Of 1 - 10 Your Rating Is?**   _____

• **Comments:** _____

_____

_____

I never ask for the customer's name, as this seems to reduce the number of responses I get back. Anonymity makes people feel free to tell you what they really think. One customer commented that he didn't like my dog, but everything else was fine!

Chapter 16: Keeping It All Together

As the proud owner of a home-based typing/word processing business, you will naturally take great care of your equipment, your reputation and your family. The one area that often gets the least amount of attention, and probably requires the most, is you. *You are the business.* And just as your former employer gave you sick days, vacation days and holidays off, you must remember to do the same thing for yourself.

One of the biggest complaints I hear from other home workers is that they seem to be working all the time. It's easy to do, because as soon as a great idea pops into you head *(usually around 3 a.m.)* you can run down the hall and write it on your bulletin board. Not only does this kind of tunnel vision sap your creative energy, you can easily loose your perspective on work versus the rest of your life.

All of the wonderful reasons that led you to decide to work from home become faint memories if you don't make a concerted effort to separate your work and leisure time. Just as my friend who leaves home every morning and reenters through another door to begin his work day, I have a similar trick. Unless I'm on deadline, I try to end my workday at 6 p.m.

That's the time I used to get home from work, and my own body rhythm seems to considerably slow down then too. So at roughly 5:45, I turn off my computer, make my "TO DO" list for the next day, straighten my office, turn out the lights and close the door. But it doesn't end there. I walk out the front door and take a brisk twenty or thirty minute walk around the neighborhood. Even during the dark winter afternoons, the cool air seems to rejuvenate me and reset my mental clock. I get back just about the time my husband is arriving home from work, and our evening together begins.

Another situation you need to become aware of is the newfound freedom to open the refrigerator door at any time during the day and eat. This can be very dangerous. When I first began working at home, I gained a pound a week for the first three months. Yikes! That's twelve pounds! I've since learned that if I don't keep those things in the house that I love to munch *(salty and crunchy)* from a bag while working, I don't have any trouble keeping my weight under control.

If you find yourself heading to the kitchen more often than necessary, try keeping a good supply of bottled water, diet sodas and fruit on hand. I've found that for my lunch break, the low calorie - low fat frozen entrees are great because I don't have to actually fix anything, I can just pop it in the microwave. That with a piece of fruit and a glass of milk keeps me happy until dinner.

As hard as you will try to set a routine work schedule, accept the fact that being at home does have some built in obstacles. Learn to be flexible, especially where your family is concerned. If your teen age daughter comes home from school obviously upset (and most of them are!) stop working and spend some time with her. Remember, one of the main reasons you decided to work for yourself is so that you can be more available to those you love. After the crisis has passed, you can always pick up where you left off, even it it's at ten o'clock that night when everyone else is in bed.

Make your work schedule work for *you*. If you need a nap in the afternoon, take one. If you wake up at 4:30 in the morning thinking about the project you're working on and can't go back to sleep, get up and go to work. If you work straight through, by noon you'll have put in a full day and you can go to the beach and read, or take a nap!

Knowing that some days you'll be able to breeze through whatever you have to do, and others will feel like torture, will help you keep work in perspective. If it's going well, you can expect to do between 30 and 50 pages of typing (double spaced), working from handwritten copy. You can probably do more if the original copy is typed and has the corrections already marked on the page.

When It Becomes Overwhelming

Train yourself to work at a relaxed and reasonable pace. Don't turn into the most demanding boss you've ever had. When work seems overwhelming and your once manageable life appears to be skidding out of control, try one, or maybe all of the following surefire remedies:

- Take A Walk
- Spend An Hour In Your Garden
- Take A Hot Bath, Sauna Or Spa Break
- Go Play Your Favorite Sport
- Take Your Dog For A Walk In The Park
- Buy Yourself A Present
- Go To A Movie Or Ball Game, Or Museum
- Have Some Fun
- Enjoy Yourself!

Whatever you're worried about will probably still be there when you return. The only difference is that you'll be able to handle it.

One of my most prized office possessions is a tape by Dr. Paul Tuthill titled *Creativity* (Mind Communications, Inc. 800-237-1974). It's part of his *"Subliminal Life Improvement Program"* and the instructions say to play it for one hour a day, for thirty days. Supposedly the hidden (time compressed) messages will bring out your creativity. My husband gave me this tape when I was in the middle of the worst writer's block imaginable. I don't have any idea what messages are hidden behind the lovely harp and flute music, what I do know is that I play this tape nonstop, every moment I'm working in my office. Maybe it's a placebo. I don't care. It soothes me, it keeps me flowing, and most of all *it works!*

When the Honeymoon Seems Over

Part of the thrill of setting up your new home business is the newness of it all. So many things to do, to buy, to decide. It's exhilarating! Then, you finally get the doors open for business, your client list grows, you're making money, and what once seemed a grand adventure starts to feel routine. Oh no! *That's one of the main reasons you left the corporate world.*

Not to worry. Every home-based entrepreneur faces this, and gets through it. Think of it like an overnight stomach flu. It feels awful, but you know that it will pass. Keep a close eye on the types of work you are involved in. If statistical typing makes you crazy, wean yourself away from those types of long-term projects. If what you really love to do is manuscript typing and editing, focus on developing a clientele that will enable you to do what you like and what you're good at.

Your word processing business is very similar to a marriage. You'll have good times and not so good. There will be days when you can't wait to get to work, and other days you'll wonder why you ever wanted to be in business for yourself! Try and keep a larger view of your work. It's only a fraction of who you are as a person.

Also try and remember other jobs you've had. Every day wasn't wonderful, and neither will they be now just because you happen to be self-employed. Enjoy the good days, and at the end of a bad one, just close the door. *Tomorrow is a new day and you just never know what's going to happen!*

Your Future Looks Bright!

I'd like to congratulate you on your decision to take control of your professional and personal life by starting your own typing/word processing business. It's a big commitment and it takes a lot of courage and dedication. You've joined the ranks of men and women of all ages, races and educational levels who will determine the way business is conducted in the next century.

With the advances in home office technology, and a universal acceptance of a new way of looking at work this is the most exciting time to have embarked on your adventure. It's easy to keep doing what you've always done, to never challenge yourself.

Grandma Moses began painting at age seventy-six, and painted every day until her one hundred and first birthday. Of her work she said, *"I look back on my life like a good day's work; it was done and I feel satisfied with it. I was happy and contented, I knew nothing more and made the best out of what life offered. And life is what we make it, always has been, always will be."*

Becoming a home-based entrepreneur is exciting and scary at the same time. Just remember that you're in good company, that there are millions of people just like you facing the same challenges every day. You can do this!

It will be very important for you to develop a support network of other home-based business owners. There's safety in numbers, and it's always a relief to be able to pick up the phone and ask someone *"How do you .....?"* You can be sure that someone, somewhere has faced the same questions you face, and has the answers.

Just because you work at home by yourself, don't ever feel that you are alone. There are hundreds of organizations able to support you and tell you where to find the information or resources you need. *(And be sure to use the Resources section at the back of this book.)*

This might be a good time for you to think about forming a local home-based business group in your community (if there isn't one already) to meet on a monthly basis. You could narrow it down to people that do basically the same type of work that you do, or open it up to anyone who works at home.

The remainder of this book is devoted to helping you locate whatever you may need to keep your business running smoothly. Keep it on your desk as a handy guide when you find you don't have the answer to your questions. Remember, someone, somewhere does!

Conclusion

Now that you've just about finished reading *How To Make Money Typing*, you should have a relatively complete idea of what is in volved in creating and running this type of home-based business. You've made a good beginning. You've answered many questions and made preliminary decisions about the type of customers you'll seek, your hours of operation, advertising, record keeping and customer service.

As can often happen with a new venture of any kind, the information can seem so overwhelming that you may have the desire to put the book aside for "later." Allowing the information in this book time to settle in you mind is actually a very good idea. We've given you a great deal to think about and a lot of information to absorb. Try not to feel that you must understand every idea, or make a decision about every facet of your new business right now. All things take time. I know it did for me.

It may be wise to set a future date for opening your door to customers. While it's true that many home-based businesses are conceived and opened within a very short period of time, don't allow yourself to feel undue pressure to begin your typing business until you are comfortable and sure that all is in place.

All great ideas deserve time to be nurtured. After finishing your reading, you may want to keep your dream of a home-based typing business all to yourself for awhile. I once heard author Ray Bradbury give a lecture on creativity, and the thing that has stayed with me all these years was his statement about nurturing and protecting your ideas. He believed that the more you talk about an idea, the less energy you have to put it into motion. He said that ideas are like babies that need care and attention from their mother.

So while it's fine to share your idea about opening a typing service, in the beginning try not to talk about it to the point that it loses its newness. You could easily talk yourself out of the dream, especially if not everyone around you shares your enthusiasm. Give yourself time to become committed and energized about the idea, then start getting feedback from people who you trust, and who you know have your best interests at heart.

It's roughly thirty months into the economic recovery of the United States, and many Americans are realizing that the dream of the great American job is gone. In its place is a new world of work. Even with the renewed growth in the economy, all sorts of people who never thought they'd be unemployed—managers, highly skilled technicians and long-seniority office workers—are looking for jobs and not finding them.

We discussed many of the reasons people have moved from a corporate culture into home-based employment, and I hope that this book has given you the information necessary for you to feel confident that this type of professional future can work for you. Home-based professional services are not just some sort of temporary fad—indeed, they are the vision of our future working environment.

Who ever would have thought that when Christopher Latham Sholes patented the first typewriter in 1868, that 125 years later a person could still earn a living using the very same principle! While technology has advanced in many areas, typing remains a constant. It's comforting to realize that people and their motivations are what truly make the world go 'round.

It will be your motivation that propels your home-based business venture forward. The variables are great and will allow you to decide how much and when you want to work; how much money you need to earn, and whether you will at some point want to expand your business into a retail location, with other people doing the actual typing. But the surest road to success is to take your time and gather as much information as you need to feel comfortable making decisions about your life and business.

This book is designed to give you a broad look at running a home-based typing service. There are many other sources to explore which will lead you to an even greater understanding of the subject. Use the Resources section at the end of the book as a starting place for doing additional reading and research in your quest to become as knowledgeable as possible about all aspects of self-employment.

Keep a folder handy in which you can place newspaper and magazine articles that you come across regarding topics related to a home-based business. This would be a good time to subscribe to one of the many magazines devoted entirely to self-employment, professional development and success, and the whole field of entrepreneurship. When you've finished reading this book, take a look at the Glossary and write down the terms you need more information on. Then plan a trip to your local library and spend an afternoon looking over books that pertain to those subjects. Research will give you the knowledge you need to make good decisions about your new venture. The more you understand, the more empowered you will feel about going into business for yourself.

Who knows where this adventure will lead. You may decide to keep your present job and run your typing service as an additional source of income. Maybe then all the money you make can be safely tucked away for your children's college education, or a dream vacation, or even to remodel your home.

Then again, your typing business may become so large that you'll soon find yourself unable to keep up with the number of clients you have and decide to subcontract some of the work to another typist. Growing your business is always a future option. You may even want to begin visualizing your business in an office building with many employees, if this is what you want to happen.

Between college semesters Joanne Thornton needed to earn some extra money, but didn't want to work full-time. She saw an ad in the Classifieds for a large office complex that wanted someone to answer their switchboard, and in exchange the different businesses within the building would pay her for her typing services. They also offered her free advertising to draw other typing clients to her, and provided all the office equipment.

Joanne soon had a thriving typing service operating. She became so busy she barely had time to answer the phone! She decided to let her return to college wait awhile. She decided to keep typing and managed to save enough money so that when she did return to school, she didn't have to work at all.

With the information this book has provided, this would be a good time to let your imagination roam a bit and see what you come up with for your own future. The wonderful thing about taking charge of your future is that almost anything is possible. You only need to discover what your desires are, then create a plan for making your life what you want it to be.

We often let ourselves get into a mental rut, thinking that what we are doing right now, the same things we've always done, are all that we're capable of doing. Whether by circumstance or design, you do have the power to change whatever no longer suits you. Life is ever changing and knowing that we can change right along with it gives us a sense of hope for the future. The big difference is whether we decide to make those changes, or allow things to remain the same.

A perfect example of accepting change and making the most of opportunity is Helen Gurley Brown, one of the most inspirational women of our century. Born in the small town of Green Forest, Arkansas in 1922, there weren't many options for women in those days. Beginning in 1942, Ms. Brown held seventeen secretarial jobs before winning a Glamour magazine contest which made her a copywriter. She wrote her first book in 1962, and was named Editor-in-Chief of Cosmopolitan magazine in 1965, a position she still holds today.

Life was never easy for this pioneer, as was explained in her 1976 book *Yesterday's Child,* a beautiful story about her retarded daughter. I chose Helen Gurley Brown as an example because she defies the stereotyping that many people associate with age, education, or cultural opportunities. She works as hard today as she did fifty years ago, and allows no one and no thing to stand in the way of her progress. Her outlook is broadened by exposing herself to new and challenging situations, a lesson for all of us.

Think of your desire to own a typing/word-processing business as just the beginning of a great, new adventure. It could be the beginning of an entirely new way of life for you. You can be sure that you will be continually challenged, because every day is a new opportunity. You'll never know who might walk through your door, and what opportunity that person will present you with. Take the challenge, let it lead you wherever it may ..... *let your new adventure begin! Good Luck!*

Resources

Associations & Organizations

American Association of Home-Based Business
PO Box 10023
Rockville, MD 20849
(301) 921-9022
AAHBB provides business support and development services to members.

American Business Women's Association
9100 Ward Parkway
PO Box 8728
Kansas City, MO 64114-0728
(816) 361-6621
ABWA is a nationwide organization offering business resources and educational programs to its members. Local chapters emphasize networking and support. Membership fees are $45/first year, $27/each successive year.

American Home Business Association
4505 Wasatch Blvd.
Salt Lake City, UT 84124
(801) 273-5455
AHBA provides home business owners with support and networking services, endorses benefits packages, and publishes *Home Business News* magazine. There is a one-time enrollment fee of $149, with quarterly dues of $29.95.

Association for Women in Computing
41 Sutter St. Suite 1006
San Francisco, CA 94104
(415) 905-4663
This association promotes the education and advancement of women in computing fields, offering conferences, workshops, and both national and regional seminars. Membership fees are $60/year.

LeTip, International
4901 Morena Blvd., Suite 703
San Diego, CA 92117
(800) 255-3847 FAX: (619) 275-0681
LeTip is a business networking organization with over 400 chapters nationwide. Members meet weekly to exchange leads and referrals. Membership dues vary; most are between $200 and $275 yearly.

Leads Club
PO Box 279
Carlsbad, CA 92018-0279

(619) 434-3761 (800) 783-3761
FAX: (619) 729-7797
Leads is a non-competitive networking organization, with 300
chapters nationwide. Members
exchange leads and referrals with
oneanother at weekly meetings.
Members pay a $75 registration
fee, then pay $21 monthly. There
is a discount if fees are prepaid.

Mother's Home Business Network
PO Box 423
East Meadow, NY 11554
(516) 997-7394 FAX: (516) 997-0839
This group caters to home-working
mothers, offering advice and
support, as well as information on
products and services of use to at-
home workers. Members pay $35
for a 16-month membership,
which includes 4 issues of
Homeworking Mothers newsletter.

National Association of Desktop Publishers
462 Old Boston St.
Topsfield, MA 01983
(508) 887-7900 x110
FAX: (508) 887-6117
This association maintains a job
bank and a referral program, as
well as offers information, support,
and discounted software and
books for those in desktop publishing fields. Members pay $95
yearly and receive NADP's bimonthly newsletter.

National Association of Home-Based Businesses
PO Box 30220
Baltimore, MD 21270
(410) 363-3698
This is a clearinghouse for information on home-based businesses,
providing specific regional resources and contacts for each
profession. The information is
targeted by region and profession, and many professional
groups maintain networking
circles. Fees vary depending on
information accessed.

National Association of Secretarial Services
3637 Fourth St. North, Suite 330
St. Petersburg, FL 33704
(813) 823-3646 FAX: (813) 894-1277
NASS offers co-op advertising,
discounted publications, and free
consultation services to its members. Members pay $120/year or
$70/semiannually.

National Association for the Self-Employed
PO Box 612067
Dallas, TX 75261-2067
(800) 232-6273
FAX: (800) 551-4446
This non-profit association endorses health benefits to members, as well as offers free legal
and consulting services, equipment leasing, and discounted

office supplies. Members pay $72/year or $169/three years.

National Association of Women Business Owners
1100 Wayne Ave. Suite 830
Silver Spring, MD 20910
(301) 608-3490
FAX: (301) 608-2596
NAWBO's aim is to network women who own their own businesses, to share common experiences and broaden the opportunities available to women business owners.

National Federation of Independent Business (NFIB)
53 Century Blvd., Suite 300
Nashville, TN 37214
(615) 872-5800
FAX: (615) 872-5899
NFIB acts primarily as a lobbying organization, supporting legislation favorable to small, independent businesses. Members receive *Independent Business* magazine. Membership dues are variable, but the minimum membership fee is $100.

The Business Network, Int'l
268 South Bucknell Ave.
Claremont, CA 91711-4907
(800) 825-8286
FAX: (909) 625-9671
This is a referral organization using "word-of-mouth marketing" to expand business for members. The organization presently runs 300 chapters, which meet regularly to exchange contacts and business. Membership is $195/year.

Professional Secretaries International
PO Box 20404
Kansas City, MO 64195-0404
(816) 891-6600
FAX: (816) 891-9118
This group, started in 1942, provides networking and support, as well as professional development programs for those in secretarial fields. Annual membership dues range from $48 to $90, varying by chapter.

U.S. Small Business Administration
500 West Madison St., Suite 1250
Chicago, IL 60661-2511
(312)353-4528
FAX: (312) 886-5688
Toll-free help desk: (800) 827-5722
SBA offers business development programs, loan programs, and business counseling services.

Periodicals & Newsletters

Brabec's National Home Business Report/Self-Employed Survival Letter
PO Box 2137-HMM5
Naperville, IL 60567
(708) 717-0488
A bimonthly newsletter offering news, information, and guidance for home-based business owners. $29/year.

The Guerrilla Marketing Newsletter
PO Box 1336
Mill Valley, CA 94942
(415) 381-8361 (800) 748-6444
A bimonthly newsletter containing innovative marketing techniques for the small business. $49/year.

Home-Based Business News
0424 S.W. Pendleton
Portland, OR 97201
(503) 246-3452
FAX: (503)452-2335
A bimonthly newspaper for homebased businesses, with columns, articles and advertising addressing the interests and needs of the home-based business community. HBBN is a regional paper, so while the articles and columns are of general interest, the advertising targets primarily the greater Portland area. $20/year.

Home-Based Business Newsletter
5114 Balcones Woods Dr. #307-231
Austin, TX 78759
(512) 258-1567
A monthly newsletter offering marketing ideas, and general advice and information for home-based business owners. $18/year.

Home Business Express
Integrity Communications
PO Box 1125
Ames, IA 50014-1125
(515) 292-7154
A monthly newsletter providing communication and networking for Iowan home workers. $30/year.

Home Office Computing
c/o Scholastics, Inc.
555 Broadway
New York, NY 10012
(800) 288-7812
A monthly magazine for small at-home businesses. Also available at newsstands. $2.95/issue or $19.97/year.

Home Office Connection
KL Publications
4003 Forest Dr.
Aliquippa, PA 15001
(412) 375-7331
A monthly newsletter designed to help the home-based typist or resume writer run a professional business. $12/year.

Home Office Opportunities
PO Box 780
Lyman, WY 82937-0780
(307) 786-4513
A bimonthly newsletter providing information and business contacts to home office owners. $18/year.

Homebased
450 Lexington Ave.
Grand Central PO
Box 2614
New York, NY 10163-2614
A bimonthly newsletter providing advice, information, and connection with other home-based business owners. $18/year.

HomeWorking
Essence Communications
1500 Broadway
New York, NY 10036
(212) 642-0600
FAX: (212) 921-5173
Monthly newsletter containing information for existing home-based businesses or those just starting up. $15/year.

Homeworking Mothers
Mother's Home Business Network
PO Box 423
East Meadow, NY 11554
(516) 997-7394
FAX: (516) 997-0839
A quarterly periodical for mothers who work at home. Free with MHBN membership.

The Newsletter on Newsletters
The Newsletter Clearinghouse
PO Box 311
Rhinebeck, NY 12572
(914)876-2081
FAX: (914) 976-2561
This newsletter provides advice and information for producers of newsletters. Delivered twice monthly. $144/year.

Svoboda's Home and Small Business
1440 W. Pratt Blvd #1
Chicago, IL 60626
(312) 764-1274
FAX: (312) 764-5931
A free monthly magazine offering advertising and information for Mid-Western area small business owners. Mailed subscriptions are $18/year.

Typing Service
American Business Directories, Inc.
5711 S. 86th Circle
Box 24737
Omaha, NE 68127
(402) 593-4600
FAX: (402) 331-5481
An informational directory listing nearly 4000 typing services. $160/copy.

Word Processing Service
American Business Directories, Inc.
5711 S. 86th Circle
Box 24737
Omaha, NE 68127
(402) 593-4600
FAX: (402) 331-5481
An informational directory listing over 7000 word processing services. $280/copy.

Working from Home
PO Box 1722
Hallandale, FL 33008
(305) 454-7216
A newsletter with advice and information for at-home workers.

Publications

The Complete Work-At-Home Companion. Herman Holtz. (Ballentine Publications, 1994) 2nd ed.
175 5th Ave.
New York, NY 10010
(800) 221-7945
This is a general resource guide to all aspects of running a business at home.

Finding Your Niche...Marketing Your Professional Service. Bart Brodsky and Janet Geis. (Community Resource Institute, Inc., 1992)
Community Resource Institute
PO Box 7880
Berkeley, CA 94709
(800) 345-0096
This book emphasizes creative ways to find a market for unique or start-up business services.

Getting Business to Come to You. Paul and Sarah Edwards, and Laura Clampitt Douglas. (Jeremy P. Tarcher, Inc., 1991)
Jeremy P. Tarcher, Inc.
5858 Wilshire Blvd., Suite 200
Los Angeles, CA 90036
(800) 847-5515
A guide to promoting a small business, with emphasis on networking, getting referrals, public relations, and advertising.

The Home Office and Small Business Answer Book. Janet Attard. (Henry Holt, 1993)
Henry Holt
115 W. 18th Street
New York, NY 10011
(800) 488-5233
In a question and answer format, this is a very accessible guide to starting-up, equipping, and marketing a small business.

Homemade Money. Barbara Brabec. (Betterway Books, 1994) 5th ed.

> Betterway Books
> 1507 Dana Ave.
> Cincinnati, OH 45207
> (800) 289-0963

The "definitive" general guide to starting and maintaining a home business.

How to Open and Operate a Home-Based Secretarial Services Business. Jan Melnik. (Globe Pequot Press, 1994)

> Globe Pequot Press
> PO Box 833
> Old Saybrook, CT 06475
> (800) 243-0495

Marketing on a Shoestring. Jeff Davidson. (John Wiley and Sons, 1994)

> John Wiley and Sons
> 605 3rd Ave.
> New York, NY 10158-0012
> (800) 225-5945

This book specializes in advising sales strategies for small businesses that have very little money to spend on marketing, including advice on creating effective ads, graphics, business cards, and directory listings.

Marketing Strategies for Small Businesses: Practical Marketing Techniques and Tactics. Richard F. Gerson. (Crisp Publications, 1994)

> Crisp Publications
> 1200 Hamilton Court
> Menlo Park, CA 94025
> (800) 442-7477

The Office Equipment Advisor. John Derrick. (What to Buy for Businesses, 1994) 2nd ed.

> What to Buy for Businesses, Inc.
> PO Box 22857
> Santa Barbara, CA 93121
> (800) 345-0096

A comprehensive guide to a variety of office equipment, evaluated for reliability, value, service, and where and how to buy.

Small-Time Operator: How To Start Your Own Small Business, Keep Your Books, Pay Your Taxes, and Stay Out of Trouble!. Bernard Kamoroff. (Bell Springs Publishing, 1990).

> Bell Springs Publishing
> PO Box 640
> Bell Springs Rd.
> Laytonville, CA 95454
> (707) 984-6746

Published by a CPA, this is a detailed and informative guide to all financial aspects of running a small business, including billing, bookkeeping and taxes.

Word Processing Plus: Profiles of Home-Based Success. Marcia Hodson. (CountrySide Publications, 1991)

> CountrySide Publications
> PO Box 115
> Galveston, In 46932
> (219) 626-2131

Forty-four women in at-home word processing professions share their experiences and advice on running a successful business.

The Work at Home Sourcebook. Lynie Arden. (Live Oak Publications, 1994)
5th ed.

> Live Oak Publications
> PO Box 2193
> Boulder, CO 80306
> (303) 447-1087

This book contains listings for many companies who hire at-home workers. The "Computer-Based Opportunities" and "Opportunities in Office Support" chapters contain many word-processing assignments; however, many of these are available only in specific regions.

Working from Home: Everything You Need to Know About Living and Working Under the Same Roof. Paul and Sarah Edwards. (Jeremy P. Tarcher, Inc., 1994) 4th ed.

> Jeremy P. Tarcher, Inc.
> 5858 Wilshire Blvd., Suite 200
> Los Angeles, CA 90036
> (800) 847-5515

The Edwardses are considered the "gurus of the home office," and their encyclopedic guide offers practical advice on creating and sustaining an at-home business.

Typical Examples of Typing Work

The following organizations use a limited number of at-home typists on a contract basis for both regular and overflow work. Most work is available only in specific regions.

Ability Group
1730 Rhode Island Ave. NW
Suite 704
Washington D.C. 20006
Transcription of medical and legal tapes. Overflow work is open to experienced professionals in the D.C. area only.

American Express Bank, Ltd.
American Express Plaza
New York, NY 10004
Word processing and transcription work for handicapped and disabled workers in the New York area.

American Stratford
Box 8128
Brattleboro, VT 05304
Typesetting work for local residents.

Appalachian Computer Services
Highway 25 South
PO Box 140
London, KY 40741
ACS employs cottage workers as employees, not independent contractors. Part-time work is available to London area residents.

Beljan, Ltd.
2870 Baker Rd.
Dexter, MI 48130
Overflow typesetting work with a book typographer. Local residents only.

Bionic Fingers
312 South Adams #3,
Glendale, CA 91205
Medical transcription work available to experienced workers living reasonably near the Glendale area.

Bureau of Office Services, Inc.
361 S. Frontage Rd.
Suite 125
Burr Ridge, IL 60521
Typing, word-processing, and

transcription work for experienced workers in the Chicago area.

Business Graphics
3314 Vassar Dr. NE
Albuquerque, NM 87107
Typesetting work for local residents.

California Typing Exchange
PO Box 3547
Hayward, CA 94540
Typists and transcribers for large metropolitan areas of California.

Carlisle Communications
442 Chavenelle Rd.
Dubuque, IA 52001
Typesetting work for Dubuque area residents.

David C. Cook Publishing Co.
850 North Grove Ave.
Elgin, IL 60120
Typing work for local residents.

Direct Data
1215 Francis Dr.
Arlington Heights, IL 60005
Word processing for experienced workers. Workers must use a personal computer and be local residents.

Green's Machines, Ltd.
1060 North 47th St.
Milwaukee, WI 53208
Word processing and transcription work, especially for Wisconsin, Kansas, and California residents.

Index Research Services
1 Waters Park Dr.
Suite 218
San Mateo, CA 94403
Part-time typing work for San Mateo and Sacramento residents.

Journal Graphics
1535 Grant St.
Denver, CO 80203
Media transcription assignments for local residents. Workers must own personal computer and modem.

Leader Typing Service
18 Caroline Ct.
North Babylon, NY 11703
Home-based typists needed for work in North Babylon region.

Letter Perfect Word Processing Center
4205 Menlo Dr.
Baltimore, MD 21215
Word processing work on mailing lists and newsletters. Available to Baltimore residents only.

Marilynn's Secretarial Service
207 E. Redwood St.
Baltimore, MD 21202
Overflow typing work for experienced PC users. Local residents only.

Mechanical Secretary
108-16 72nd Ave.
Forest Hills, NY 11375
Typing and transcribing work for residents of Manhattan, Brooklyn, or Queens.

Mod-Komp Corporation
749 Truman Ave.
East Meadow, NY 11554
Manuscript typing for computer-literate workers. Local residents only.

Network Typesetting
220 Bank of Nebraska Mall
42nd Center
Omaha, NE 68105
Typesetting input work for Omaha residents.

North Shore Medical Transcribing
18 Federal Lane
Coran, NY 11727
Transcription work for local residents with experience.

Outer Office
10005 Old Columbia Rd.
Columbia, MD 21046
Word processing work for experienced area residents.

RMS Business Services
210 West Pennsylvania Ave., Suite 30 Towson, MD 21204
Word processing work for locals with
experience.

Research Information Systems
2355 Camino Vida Roble
Carlsbad, CA 92009-1572
Medical journal indexing for experienced typists. Must own PC and live locally.

Secreteam
455 Sherman St.
Suite 120
Denver, CO 80203
Word processing and transcribing work for experienced workers with IBM PC or compatible equipment. Local residents only.

The Typing Company
PO Box 955
Davis, CA 95617
Academic and medical typing work for Davis residents only.

Glossary

Account - a term which refers to a client serviced by a business

Accounting - a method of keeping records of the financial transactions of a business

Advertising - a paid message in which a business is identified and promoted

A/V - an audiovisual presentation of both pictures and words

Broadside - a one-page promotional flyer folded for mailing

Brochure - a small booklet promoting a service or product

Budget - a plan for spending a certain amount of money

Business plan - a written map or guide of how a business is designed to operate

Business-to-Business advertising - services or products designed to sell to other businesses

Cable Television - paid subscriber programming, often with advertising for local businesses

Call Waiting - a telephone feature that lets you know when another caller is on the line

Campaign - a coordinated advertising promotion plan

Chamber of Commerce - an organization whose purpose is to support the small business owners in a community

Classified Advertising - a small line or display ad often seen in the back of a newspaper

Client - a customer who uses your services or products

Cold Calling - using the telephone to solicit a customer one has never spoken to before

Collateral - printed information about products, such as catalogs, direct mail, brochures and fliers

Confidentiality - keeping client information within the confines of the office

Contract - the written agreement for work performed and money to be paid for that work

Copy - the text of written material

DBA - Doing Business As, a business using a fictitious name

Deadline - the time at which a project must be finished as agreed

Dedicated word processor - a computer designed to produce typed documents, retrieved from an internal storage system

Demographics - Statistics relating to the specific characteristics of a segment of the population, e.g., age, race, sex, income

Direct Mail - advertising materials delivered by the Post Office

Display advertising - the placement of a paid ad in the newspaper, outside the classified section, to attract or inform prospective customers

Editorial - all written material of a publication that is not advertising including articles, news, briefs, etc.

Estimate - a rough guess or projection of the cost for a specific job

Ethics - the practice of honesty and integrity in work situations

Farm out - to assign work to another professional

Fax - abbreviation for facsimile, a machine that sends information, text and graphics by telephone transmission

Feature - a full-length editorial story to appear in a newspaper, magazine, or other publication

Fictitious Business Name Statement - (FBN) a legal form filed with governmental agencies for a business using a name other than that of the owners

Financing - revenue obtained for the express purpose of running a business or buying equipment

Freelancer - a self-employed professional, usually a home-based worker

Image - the public's perception of a firm, individual, or product

In-house - refers to any work performed internally by an organization

Inquiry form - information about a prospective customer's work request

Layout - a rough sketch of how a finished brochure or ad will look

Letterhead - printed stationary with a company's logo and/or name

Letter of recommendation - formal letter endorsing the work or performance of a company or individual

License - a legal permit to perform certain business functions

Logo - a company name designed with artwork or special type

List broker - an organization or individual that rents mailing lists

Mailing list - a database of names and addresses, typically consisting of customers who have purchased similar products or services in the past

Market - a specific part of the population that may become customers of a particular service or product

Marketing - various activities performed by an organization or individual to promote and sell their services and products

Marketing communications - activities relating to promoting a product or service, including public relations, sales and advertising

Media - all forms of communication that bring product or service information to the business community and the public in general

Mission statement - a written statement that concisely describes the planned business activities of a company or individual businessperson

Networking - the process of making and connecting business contacts to generate work for hire

Newsletter - a marketing material designed to give product or service information to current and potential customers

Non-profit organization - an organization designed to do specific activities which does not generate a monetary profit

Paper stock - the quality, weight and color of paper usually used in printing

Partnership - the legal agreement between two or more persons to operate a business or service oriented company

Per diem - fees charged or services performed daily

Photocopy service - a location capable of reproducing documents in either small or large quantities

Portfolio - a presentation package containing samples of work, awards, recommendations, shown to prospective clients

Press release - news or information written and sent to all media sources

Price quote - a dollar amount agreed for work to be performed

Product manager - the person responsible for the supervision of a specific product or service

Promotion - activities designed to encourage the purchase of a product or service

Prospect - a person or organization with the motivation, authority and financial resources to purchase a product or service

Public relations - any activity which causes a favorable image or story to be printed or broadcast about a company's products or services

Radio advertising - the placement and broadcast of a specific message relating to a product or service, usually 30 or 60 seconds in length

Repeat business - customers that return to buy after the initial purchase

Research - interviews, studies or surveys designed to explain how the public perceives a specific product or service

Reply card - a self-addressed, usually postage paid post card designed to get customers to respond to advertising or information

Resources - a group of institutions, persons or organizations which offer assistance and information

Sales promotion - a specific marketing effort designed to create interest and excitement about a product or service to increase sales

SBA - Small Business Administration, an organization of the United States government designed to specifically aid and encourage small business activities

Schedule - (work) the time allowed and planned to do specific projects

SCORE - Service Corps of Retired Executives, a volunteer organization that provides counseling and help to small business owners

Software - computer programs which enable a computer to do specific functions, i.e. word-processing, database management, accounting spreadsheets, etc.

Sole proprietorship - the legal ownership status of a company or business by one person only

Telemarketing - the act of selling products or services to customers over the telephone

Time management - the ability to schedule and complete pre-determined tasks

To-do list - a written document listing activities to be completed

Voice Mail - an automated answering system that records messages for later retrieval

Word processing - the act of inputting copy or information into a computer to be printed on paper

Work space - the designated area where work is to be performed

Index